Penguin Education

Penguin Modern Psychology Texts

Work and Well-being

Peter Warr and Toby Wall

Advisory Editor: B. M. Foss

Peter Warr and Toby Wall

Work and Well-being

Penguin Books

Penguin Books Ltd,
Harmondsworth, Middlesex, England
Penguin Books Inc.,
7110 Ambassador Road, Baltimore, Maryland 21207, U.S.A.
Penguin Books Australia Ltd,
Ringwood, Victoria, Australia
Penguin Books Canada Ltd,
41 Steelcase Road West, Markham, Ontario, Canada
Penguin Books (N.Z.) Ltd,
182–190 Wairau Road, Auckland 10, New Zealand

First published 1975

Made and printed in Great Britain by
Hazell Watson & Viney Ltd,
Aylesbury, Bucks
Set in Monotype Times

Contents

Preface

This book is about the quality of working life, and we approach that important topic through an examination of the work satisfaction and mental health of individual employees. Research investigations are reviewed which provide information about what people want from work and about possible ways of satisfying both their aspirations and the needs of the organization which employs them. Our interest extends to organizations of all kinds – publicly or privately owned, profit-making or not, large or small. So we shall describe studies carried out in factories, coal-mines, hospitals, offices, schools and building sites. These involve jobs at different levels – manual, clerical, professional and managerial work – but our emphasis will tend towards the jobs of lower-level employees.

Our account of well-being at work necessarily brings in questions of value as well as of fact. We are not only looking at organizations as they are now but also inquiring how they might be altered to increase the psychological health of the members. In practice, then, we are asking: what ought to happen at work? how should employees be treated? what would a job be like which met both their needs and those of the organization? It is in this sense that we are raising moral as well as practical issues.

These issues are introduced through a presentation of research evidence. This comes from several different disciplines, but our own background in psychology means that it is psychological issues and research investigations which capture most of our attention. Progress has been considerable in recent years and psychologists are making increasing contributions to practical decision-making as well as to more theoretical understanding. But any one discipline has its limits, and we have tried also to draw on material from sociology, industrial relations, organizational behaviour, management theory and elsewhere.

Our own professional activities as research and development workers in applied psychology make quite clear the difficulties of bridging the gap between theory and practice. The day-to-day requirements of meeting production targets, avoiding backlogs or reducing expenditure are very pressing. So too are the traditional ways of thinking and feeling which characterize managements, trade unions and individual employees. These various factors are typically in multiple conflict with each other, leading to immense difficulties in the introduction of change. The research worker needs to become more involved in these ongoing practical problems if his impact is to be widespread. This means a greater emphasis on what has been called 'action research', extending sometimes into development studies whose emphasis upon innovation perhaps justifies the label 'research action'. These practical activities do however need to be complemented by essentially scientific appraisals of the state of knowledge at any one time. This book aims to be such an appraisal.

It has taken well over a year to write, interrupted by many other activities. During this period page upon page of typing and retyping have passed through the hands of June Goodram and Karen Thompson. Reinforcements were even necessary in the shape of Carol Jones and Flavia Shrivastava. Our thanks go to them, and to colleagues in the Social and Applied Psychology Unit of Sheffield University for patient and helpful advice about issues that have troubled us over the months.

1 Psychological well-being at work

Societies are to be measured in terms of their psychological as well as their material success. It has now become customary to record and compare material development in terms of output-per-head, energy consumed, level of affluence, numbers of motorcars and so on, but the psychological quality of society is less easily documented. Several different perspectives are possible, in terms of psychological illnesses, artistic standards, moral codes, criminal statistics, community projects and the like. One particularly important perspective of this kind is in terms of how members of society organize themselves in their occupational life: how is individual well-being influenced by the institutions of employment?

The chapters of this book are addressed to that question, and it is as well to make clear at the outset that it is a question of value as well as of fact. Attempts to understand and increase psychological well-being include attempts to make sense of what people could or should be as well as what they are. In some areas there is clear agreement on issues of value (people should generally be happy rather than unhappy, for instance), but in many specific circumstances there is room for disagreement and discussion. This will become clear as the book proceeds, but the general value-orientation underlying its approach should be stated here: we believe that it is morally desirable for work to be such that people like it, and also that members of society in different positions and at different levels should be taking more active steps to make it likeable. Such an approach derives additional force from recent government reports in several countries which have suggested that the quality of working life is often lower than many feel to be appropriate (e.g. US Department of Health, Education and Welfare, 1973; Wilson, 1973).

Work is a central part of life and of society. Work organizations make society what it is and, conversely, they are made by society. The vast majority of us will always have to provide for ourselves, either directly as did our prehistoric ancestors or indirectly through contributions to society which are rewarded by support and income. Furthermore our occupational life is organized in many ways to satisfy our requirements for companionship, achievement and gain: people are aware of positive benefits in working which extend well beyond a grudging acceptance of its necessity. Most people would continue working even if they could afford not to (Morse and Weiss, 1955), and many find a sense of individual purpose in their work. Maslow, a leading humanistic psychologist whose views will be discussed at several points later, has said: 'I think I am just most happy and most fulfilled, and most myself, and most being as if that's what I were meant to be when I am involved in my work' (Frick, 1971, p. 31).

It is not only the intellectual commentators who stress the value of work. A steelworker writes: 'The open-hearth furnaces served me well and I served them well, and I'm not sorry we met. They gave me the chance of a worth-while working life in a tremendously interesting industry' (Fraser, 1969, p. 68). Another working man reports: 'I am not sorry to have spent eighteen of my thirty-eight years as a bricklayer. There is a certain joy in being able to do something competently with one's hands and of using muscular force with common sense to overcome obstacles, to exercise individual initiative' (Fraser, 1969, p. 145). The pleasures of using practised skills are emphasized by a toolmaker describing how he developed his abilities with guidance from an experienced colleague: 'My personality underwent a change which reflected this situation in creating something. It gave me the instinct for creative work, and the realization that in work alone can personal fulfilment be found. The craftsman is not *socially* superior because he can perform a given task which others cannot, but he is *personally* superior because within his work he can find himself. The tragedy of most industrial occupations is their inability to afford satisfaction at this personal level' (Fraser, 1969, p. 27).

That last statement is an important one, though it might be expanded to cover other pleasures of a more social kind. Work matters to people, and as happens with other salient parts of their lives they develop mixed feelings about it. They love and they hate their work. These comments from an unemployed man say it well:

> Frankly, I hate work. Of course, I could say with equal truth that I love work; that it is a supremely interesting activity; that it is often fascinating; that I wish I didn't have to do it; that I wish I had a job at which I could earn a decent wage. That makes six subjective statements about work and all of them are true for me.
>
> I could tell of my experiences of being a miner, for mining is the work I've mostly done. The crudity, dirt, pain, the hazards and dreary monotony, the often back-breaking toil of mining are things I know about.
>
> I also know about the hopes and fears and the struggles of miners; their casual everyday courage, their uninhibited humour, their tremendous dignity and their almost unbelievable propensity for profanity, rich, colourful and strange in moments of crisis.
>
> If that weren't enough I could go on to say something of my experiences, which were never dull, as a bus conductor in a busy provincial city, or of those in a large engineering factory where 'union' was definitely a dirty word, and practically every single moment was as dull as ditchwater [Fraser, 1968, p. 273].

Our position is that work will always matter to people, that they will always love it and hate it, and that society, through changing the nature of some work, should help people to love it more than hate it. The necessary changes are massively complex and difficult, they are continually constrained by economic and practical considerations, and they will come about only slowly. But employees of all types and levels should consider their moral stance on the problems of work, and governments should provide a lead. Our aim in this book is to look at some research evidence, and we have marshalled this around the notion of 'psychological well-being'.

This concept requires some introduction. It often enters into discussions of the nature of health. The World Health Organization, for instance, defines health as the presence of physical and emotional well-being. Our concern will therefore be partly with issues of mental health, but because we are dealing with well-being at work attention will be limited to mental health issues in relation to what happens to people in their occupational environment. This perspective necessarily raises questions of what is often called job satisfaction – how satisfied are people with their work activities? Let us provisionally suggest that in its scope the concept of psychological well-being at work stands somewhere between those of mental health in general and job satisfaction in particular.

The central part of the first chapter is an examination of the similarities and differences between these three notions. We are principally concerned with them as valued states in themselves, but a second reason for their study should also be indicated. Is it not the case that people who feel positively towards their work will be more effective at it? At the extremes of negative feeling there is clearly a link between well-being and effectiveness: consider the completely uninvolved employee who only works in response to coercion, or the overstressed executive whose performance deteriorates through failing health. More generally however the association with effectiveness can be dwarfed by differences in ability or by technological or economic conditions (cf. Herman, 1973; Wicker, 1969).

Feelings about work are particularly associated with effectiveness when performance and reward are closely dependent on each other (Porter and Lawler, 1968), when ability levels are broadly appropriate for the job (Carlson, 1969), and when people have voluntarily opted for the work they are undertaking (Doll and Gunderson, 1969). (See also Schwab and Cummings, 1970; and Slocum, 1970.) Other forms of effectiveness from the standpoint of an employing organization include whether people leave, so that recruiting and retraining become extensive; here common knowledge and research (Pettman, 1973; Vroom, 1964) agree that negative work attitudes do often influence labour turnover. A general willingness to undertake work and to accept change beyond one's narrowly prescribed duties are also expected to accompany positive feelings about the job.

Psychological well-being at work is thus to be aimed at for two reasons: as a desirable end in itself and as a means of developing more effective organizations. What should be understood by the term, and how is it related to job satisfaction?

Well-being and job satisfaction

The literature on job satisfaction is enormous both in quantity and scope. It deals with the attitudes people have towards their jobs, and the causes and consequences of these attitudes. Early research in this field tended to employ questionnaires or interviews to measure overall reactions to work rather than specified opinions about aspects of it. Hoppock (1935), for instance, took several measures of how people felt about their job as a whole. These measures included a seven-point scale from 'I love it' to 'I hate it' and another from 'no one likes his job better than I like mine' to 'no one dislikes his job more than I dislike mine'. Patterns of scores were studied and overall satisfaction shown to be related to features such as occupational level and age. Later studies of this kind have also used measures of overall satisfaction. Brayfield and Rothe (1951), for instance, required people to indicate agreement or disagreement with a series of statements, such as 'my job is like a hobby to me' and 'most of the time I have to force myself to go to work'.

As research into job satisfaction developed, measures of overall job satisfaction were complemented by more focused approaches in acknowledgement of the fact that the concept is a multidimensional one (e.g. Evans, 1969; Locke, 1975; Vroom, 1964; Wanous and Lawler, 1972). In this way for example the Job Description Index (Smith *et al.*, 1969) contains sub-scales to measure attitudes towards pay, promotion prospects, the work itself, supervision and co-workers. This index was developed for American application and a similar questionnaire standardized on British samples (Cross, 1973) has in addition a sub-scale to tap feelings about the firm as a whole. A derivative for use with managers has a seventh sub-scale to cover attitudes towards subordinates (Warr and Routledge, 1969). Many investigators feel that even the employment of seven or more sub-scales cannot do justice to the complexity of people's reactions to work, and it is usually appropriate also to apply some situation-specific measures to tap the nature of job satisfaction in a particular work-place.

Several hundred investigations have shown that in general people say that they are satisfied with their work. Such an outcome is not too surprising since strong dissatisfaction would in normal circumstances lead to a change of job, and since habit and rationalization over the years are likely to produce some kind of personal adjustment to a work situation. In this respect it is noteworthy that length of service and job satisfaction are typically associated positively (e.g. Wall, 1972), and that job level (itself linked to length of service) is a consistent predictor of satisfaction (e.g. Porter, 1962; Porter and Lawler, 1965). By way of additional illustration of job satisfaction research we may cite suggestions that satisfaction is higher in small-town factories than in those situated in large conurbations (e.g. Katzell, Barrett and Parker, 1961). Palmore's (1969a, 1969b) study is also important. He carried out a longitudinal investigation to predict the age at which people would die. His predictive variables included ratings of general physical functioning, specific indices of heart and other conditions, smoking habits, economic security, religious attitudes and so on. Several variables predicted longevity to a significant degree, but the strongest overall predictor was job satisfaction: people who felt positively towards their work were more likely to live to an older age ($r = 0{\cdot}26$, $n = 266$).

The concept of job satisfaction is clearly an interesting one, and we shall necessarily be dealing with it throughout the book. It is, however, limited, and we shall often go beyond it. In practice the emphasis of job satisfaction research has tended to be negative; the desirable state is seen as a reduction of dissatisfaction. In this way studies of satisfaction with working conditions have been addressed to the removal of unpleasant features of the environment, and dissatisfaction with superiors has been remedied by training for foremen and managers. It is only a slight caricature of many studies to suggest that the 'satisfied employee' has typically been viewed as analogous to the 'contented cow', munching its feed and producing milk with the minimum of fuss and activity.

A negative conception of satisfaction is of course partly valid. To promote job satisfaction we have to remedy environmental deficiencies (ensuring that the temperature or lighting are acceptable, for instance) and we should reduce the cause for individual complaints about too much paper-work, inadequate tools or inferior raw materials. But this only takes us some way along the road to psychological well-being. Feeling good about your job is not entirely the same as not feeling bad about it; in its full sense psychological well-being at work is a question of satisfaction-plus.

Job satisfaction and mental health

The nature of the 'plus' may be illustrated through some recent discussions of physical and mental health. In one sense we are healthy if we are not ill, and the medical profession is dedicated to our health in this negative sense of curing our illnesses. Less obviously it is also concerned with making healthy people more healthy, by extending them in various ways to increase their fitness. Positive health consists in modes of living which go beyond the mere existence implied by negative concepts of health.

The significance of this distinction for mental health and job attitudes has been forcefully argued by Herzberg (1966). His views will be examined in more detail in Chapter 2 (see pages 35 to 38), but a brief outline is appropriate here. Herzberg suggests that mental health requires two kinds of development, both an adjustment to the environment so that negative states are minimized and also the occurrence of and potential for 'psychological growth'. Herzberg describes six characteristics of psychological growth, as follows:

(1) *Knowing more*. The continuing acquisition of knowledge is said to be quite essential for psychological growth. Growth comes from exposure to the unfamiliar and novel. Herzberg

clearly has in mind both non-work and work experiences, but with regard to the latter he inquires: 'Is it not legitimate to ask, after a job assignment, whether an employee has learned anything – has he in this case added to what he knows?' (1966, p. 59).

(ii) *Relationships in knowledge.* Growth is also dependent upon an individual organizing and integrating what he is learning; an accumulation of disconnected and inapplicable facts has no value.

(iii) *Creativity.* The production of something new is viewed by Herzberg as a third salient characteristic of psychological growth. That which is created is rarely of momentous significance to mankind as a whole; the important process is the production of knowledge or things originating from within the individual.

(iv) *Effectiveness in ambiguity.* Growth requires that we are able 'to live with insecurity, to accept change and alteration, to deal with complexity' (p. 63), that we are not entirely dependent upon 'absolutes, unconditionals, perfections and predictabilities' (p. 62). 'It is a trend in modern industry to engineer all ambiguity out of jobs and render them suitable to a child's ability' (p. 65).

(v) *Individuation.* Psychological growth, as biological growth, proceeds from an undifferentiated mass to separate and distinct areas of experience and behaviour. In part this involves a separation from other people, the development of an individuality which is not overdetermined by conformity and group dependence.

(vi) *Real growth.* Herzberg's final characteristic of psychological growth is in some ways a general feature of all the others. Growth must not be false or artificial: people should know themselves as they are, not through public façades. Furthermore, 'growth at the expense of others merely diminishes them; it does not add to your psychological tissue' (p. 70).

Two points should be emphasized about Herzberg's view of positive mental health. First, he is describing aspects of life which have a generality well beyond the work situation. In doing this his concern, and ours, is to suggest that assessments of a work situation should more often include evaluations in these terms: positive mental health of employees should be one of any organization's principal objectives. The organizational constraints of work must of course moderate the potential for growth through many jobs, but these constraints themselves should be examined and their assumed validity tested.

The second point to note about Herzberg's account of psychological growth is that the concept is both multi-dimensional and value-laden. It contains several overlapping features and their definition as good is partly due to the value system of the person making the definition. This intermingling of value and fact seems to be inherent in any specification of positive health, mental or physical. It may be seen in Jahoda's (1958) review of six different approaches to the concept of mental health. These approaches are as follows:

(i) *Positive attitudes to the self.* A mentally healthy attitude to yourself is described in terms like self-acceptance, self-confidence, self-esteem or self-respect. Several features of this cluster of terms illustrated by Jahoda include an accurate understanding of yourself, a sense of identity, integration and stability, and a general positive reaction to what you experience.

(ii) *Growth, development and self-actualization.* Many writers have stressed that a strong investment-in-living represents positive health. Herzberg's account is of this kind, as is Maslow's (e.g. 1973) concern for self-actualization (see also Chapter 2, pages 32 to 35). Maslow emphasizes how we all have a potential for being more than we are at the moment, and that the realization of this potential through activities or relationships is a prime aspect of health. In a similar vein, Becker (1972, p. 154) aims for the development of free, independent, self-reliant personalities.

(iii) *Personality integration.* Jahoda summarizes a third set of prescriptions in terms of some kind of relatedness or balance within the individual. This relatedness has been seen by some in psychoanalytic terms of the ego and the id, and by others in terms of resilience of character or of the successful resolution of mental conflicts.

(iv) *Autonomy*. A fourth approach to mental health has already been illustrated in one of Herzberg's characteristics of growth. Many people have suggested that mental health involves an ability to resist environmental influences, to energize and steer yourself rather than always responding to external pressures.

(v) *Perception of reality*. Herzberg also exemplifies the writers whom Jahoda characterizes as viewing mental health in terms of accurate perception of reality. In part this is a question of not allowing your perception of people and events to be too influenced by your personal attitudes and emotions, and in part it is seen as a question of sympathy and concern – recognizing that other people and their experiences are worthy of your interest and attention.

(vi) *Environmental mastery*. This last approach to mental health in Jahoda's summary is related to several of the others. Health is seen in terms of an acceptable degree of success in different spheres – interpersonal relations, problem-solving, work and so on. The mentally healthy person is someone who achieves at least some of his goals in areas which are important to him.

The third writer on mental health to be discussed is particularly concerned with what happens at work. Kornhauser (1965, p. 38) echoes several themes presented so far: 'An adequate conceptualization of good mental health refers to something more than passive adjustment, contentment, 'homeostatic balance', and freedom from inner tensions. Few people would accept the healthy vegetable as a model. The more positive aspects of mental health, the active efforts of people to cope with their world, surely deserve attention'. Kornhauser's own definition of mental health contains six interrelated elements – level of manifest anxiety and emotional tensions, degree of self-esteem, degree of interpersonal hostility, degree of sociability, level of overall satisfaction with life and level of personal morale. He measured each of these through structured interviews with a sample of manual workers and investigated their association with traditional indices of job satisfaction.

This study will be examined in Chapter 6 (pages 121 to 122). For the present we wish to stress the central theme of Kornhauser's work. This flows from the sixth issue in Jahoda's summary, above: 'Mental health depends above all else on the development and retention of goals that are neither too high nor too low to permit realistic, successful maintenance of belief in one's self as a worthy, effective human being, a useful and respected member of society' (Kornhauser, 1965, p. 14).

> Industrial workers, like all the rest of us, are caught on the horns of a dilemma: if they want *too much* relative to what they are prepared to strive for with some degree of success, the result is defeat and frustration; if they want *too little*, the consequence is a drab existence devoid of colour, exhilaration, and self-esteem. Good mental health demands a middle course [p. 270].

This idea is reflected in many of the definitional characteristics mentioned earlier. Mental health requires that we want to be more than we are at present or to achieve more than we do at present. And some degree of satisfaction of these wants is essential for our self-esteem. Psychological well-being arises from our wants and is evidenced in our self-esteem.

The notion of a 'want' is central to discussions of well-being and will recur throughout the following chapters. The concept is part of a cluster of ideas including satisfaction, preference, attractiveness, liking, interest, pleasure, desire, goal and others that are generically associated with the concept of 'motivation'. Much psychological work in this area has been aimed at the causal explanation and prediction of exhibited behaviour, and there has been only limited research interest in the experienced features of motivation, in people's feelings associated with their motive states.

Psychological well-being at work is only attainable if some satisfaction is obtained from your own actions, so that in this book we are of course interested in work *behaviour*. But our intention is to give rather less emphasis to behaviour than is often the case and rather more to the experiences of work. These central experiences of motives will be referred to as wants, and our main concern will be to understand the nature and development of wants in the work situation. Not all wants can be translated into action, but their intensity and degree of satisfaction are essential to psychological well-being.

This theme will be developed throughout the book, and a more explicit theoretical formulation will be presented in the final chapter (see pages 168 to 177). At that point also the links between wanting and self-esteem will be discussed further (pages 177 to 182). For the present it should be noted that the intensity of wants is variable from situation to situation (as for example your feelings of hunger or your desire to finish a particular piece of work), but that wants can also be examined at a more dispositional level. The latter perspective is in terms of continuing motivational systems, such that one person may be seen to be by disposition a harder worker than another.

The dispositional wants, those that are relatively permanent across time and situations, have some affinity with attitudes, values and personality traits. We take these notions to be broader than the ones involved in wanting (e.g. Audi, 1972; Warr, 1975), and for practical purposes have mainly limited ourselves to an examination of want-systems at a particular moment or in a particular period. In this way we shall deal with desires for more pay at one point in time rather than with attitudes to money in general. Moreover we shall concentrate upon factors which affect the changing intensity of wants of this context-specific kind.

In summary, then, we shall be primarily concerned with the more experiential features of motivation. Changes in the intensity of these are closely linked with satisfaction and the more positive aspects of well-being, and consistencies in their intensity are associated with attitudes and personality systems. Most writers in the field of occupational and organizational psychology have inclined towards the use of the terms 'attitude' and 'satisfaction'. The first of these is too broad for our aims, and the latter gives too much weight to the negative features of motivation. For these reasons we shall also use the straightforward, four-letter, Anglo-Saxon word 'want'!

Other aspects of well-being

We have suggested that well-being at work is more than mere job satisfaction, when this is defined mainly negatively in terms of the lack of job dissatisfaction. Satisfaction is part of well-being, but the notion includes some more positive elements from within the definition of mental health. Yet the contrast between positive and negative elements should not be overdrawn. In many areas our wants are both negative and positive. For example we want to avoid unacceptable levels of stress but at the same time we may seek challenge and diversity; we do not want too much work but we may want to be kept busy. Similarly, an interest in mental health must be accompanied by a concern for mental illness. Sickness absence from work due to psychoneuroses, psychoses, nervousness, debility and headaches is increasing faster than any other form of certified absence. Mental illness in the United Kingdom claims nearly 40 million lost working days each year (National Association for Mental Health, 1971); by comparison the average annual number of days lost by strikes in the past five years is less than 15 million (Department of Employment, 1974).

Although job satisfaction, well-being and mental health are related concepts, there are certain situations where they can be negatively associated with each other. An able and trained immigrant may find himself restricted to menial work well below his previous standard, or an intelligent and keen junior manager may be constrained by his overpowering boss. In cases like these, where realistic wants and self esteem are stifled through an inappropriate arrangement of work, job satisfaction and well-being may be low; yet such a reaction on the part of the employee is not unhealthy.

Our concern with wants and well-being at work will sometimes stress studies of job satisfaction and will sometimes veer more towards the concepts of mental health. We shall largely restrict our attention to what actually goes on in a work situation. This leaves aside the complex and crucial questions of the interrelationships between work and non-work experiences. Tales of the love-sick typist are part of managerial folklore, but less considered by managers are how their overwork affects health and thus indirectly work itself or how neglect of family responsibilities can eventually influence their work and well-being. On the positive side, status within your occupation carries with it opportunities for satisfying a variety of non-work wants in society at large.

One interesting approach to well-being in general (work *and* non-work) has been reported by Bradburn (1969). He asked people questions of the following kind: 'During the past few weeks did you ever feel particularly excited or interested in something?', 'During the past few weeks did you ever feel depressed or very unhappy?' Reports of positive affect during the time period (feeling interested, etc.) were found to be uncorrelated with reports of negative affect during the same time, but the two facets of well-being were seen to be differentially related to other life experiences. For example overall job satisfaction was linked to negative affect, but not to positive affect.

In passing we should note that, just as well-being is a question of satisfaction-plus, the much-used sociological concept of 'alienation' can be viewed as dissatisfaction-minus. This concept has several aspects, notably powerlessness, meaninglessness, normlessness, isolation and self-estrangement (Pearlin, 1962; Seeman, 1959), but in practice the measurement of alienation at work tends to be in terms of how far workers are dissatisfied. Aiken and Hage (1966) introduce their study in terms of Marx's notions of alienation from the process of production and alienation from fellow workers (see Bottomore, 1963). Yet their measure of alienation from work contains six items of the kind 'How satisfied are you with your present job in the light of career aspirations?' and their index of alienation from fellow workers involves two questions: 'How satisfied are you with your supervisor?' and 'How satisfied are you with your fellow workers?' More sophisticated measures and studies of the relationships between work alienation and broader forms of societal powerlessness, meaninglessness and so on are clearly required.

The available indices of well-being are of several kinds. As was noted on page 13, most research into job satisfaction has focused on questionnaire or interview measures, but increasing attention is being paid to the examination of mental health at work. Questionnaires and structured interviews have an important place here (e.g. Kornhauser, 1965; McLean, 1970), but so too do clinical assessments by medical practitioners and evidence from physiological investigations or studies of illness distributions. Since it is the wants which people bring to their job situation that ultimately determine psychological well-being at work, we shall also be concerned with information about preferences, values, attitudes and similar emotional states. Clinical interviews conducted by appropriately trained professionals can readily tap these aspects of well-being.

The plan of the book

The four central chapters of the book (Chapters 3 to 6) will each cover one aspect of well-being. We shall in turn look at feelings about pay, interpersonal relationships, managerial practices and the job itself. Chapter 7 will deal with research into stress at work, particularly the strains arising from its social organization. In the final chapter we shall integrate some earlier themes in more general terms and make some practical suggestions for applying psychology to promote well-being at work.

We shall pay only limited attention to the more physical aspects of work such as light, noise, temperature, equipment, and so on. Knowledge about these and about ergonomic aspects of man-machine system design has been documented by Bell (1974), DeGreene (1970), Gagné (1962), Morgan *et al.* (1963), Poulton (1970), Singleton (1974), Van Cott and Kincade (1972) and others.

Our more detailed reviews of current understanding need to be set in a historical context. This is provided in Chapter 2, to which we now turn.

2 Theories of work attitudes

The acquisition and application of knowledge are in part determined by society's contemporary value systems. There are wide areas of understanding and action in which accepted truth varies from generation to generation, and doctrines about industry and its employees have both reflected and influenced more general ideologies. The changes which have occurred in industrial society's orientation to work are in this way reflected in the main themes of industrial psychology through this century. Not surprisingly these themes have progressed from the simple to the complex, but they have also shifted from a rather single-minded concern for productive efficiency and the rights of the employer to a more wide-ranging perspective which incorporates employee well-being as well as efficiency and profitability.

This chapter will examine four research themes which have influenced both thinking and practice in the organization of work. The principal spokesmen for these themes are Frederick Taylor (1856–1915), Elton Mayo (1880–1949), Abraham Maslow (1908–70) and Frederick Herzberg (born 1923).

Scientific management

The first of these theorists systematically to consider what motivated people at work was Taylor, an engineer working in American industry at the turn of the century. Taylor's main concern was to increase efficiency, and his approach, described for example in *The Principles of Scientific Management* (1911, reprinted in 1947) is of interest both because of its influence upon subsequent job attitude research and for its more general relationship to the field of industrial psychology.

The basic aim of scientific management was the development of a 'science' to replace the 'rules of thumb' typically used by managers of the day. Taylor pointed to the fact that whereas managers had reliable and useful information concerning the capacity and efficiency of their machines, they had no such information about their employees. With this in mind he focused his attention upon two problems, how to make work methods more efficient, and how to encourage men to work harder.

Taylor advocated the following procedure for improving efficiency in manual work. A number of individuals who were exceptionally skilful at the work in question were to be found, the physical movements they used were to be closely scrutinized, and each movement or unit of activity carefully timed. From all the different elementary movements demonstrated by the skilful group the most rapid, and the slowest and redundant, were to be identified Finally, a new method of working which capitalized on the rapid movements and avoided the slow and unnecessary ones was to be developed. A similar procedure was to be followed for establishing the best equipment to use during each stage of the work, and for the layout of the physical environment. Having decided the 'best method' in this manner, it was to be put into practice by training individuals in its use. The training should be so exact that every employee would carry out the same movements in the same order, hour after hour, day after day. With a number of routine manual jobs this was put into practice with spectacular effects in terms of increased output, and this aspect of Taylor's work provided the impetus for later developments in the field of work study.

Taylor appreciated, however, that the success of a method devised in this manner depended not only upon the elimination of the least efficient physical movements, but also upon the cooperation of those trained in its use. He proposed two 'laws' of human motivation which would encourage employee cooperation and which, he claimed, were derived from 'carefully planned and executed experiments extending through a term of years'. (The exact nature of these experiments, however, remains obscure.) The first of his 'laws' concerned the effect of the 'task idea' upon the individual. Taylor expressed this concept in the following way:

> ... the average workman will work with the greatest satisfaction, both to himself and his employer, when he is given each day a definite task which he is to perform in a given time, and which constitutes a proper day's work for a good workman. This furnishes the workman with a clear-cut standard, by which he can throughout the day measure his own progress, and the accomplishment of which affords him the greatest satisfaction [1947, pp. 120–21].

This notion was put into practice by giving specific production goals to each individual and by ensuring close supervision throughout the work. In today's language the 'task idea' is similar to 'feedback', 'knowledge of results' or 'role clarity'. The second 'law' concerned the economic returns the individual obtained from work. Taylor argued that employees would only work at their best speed if they were assured of a 'large and permanent increase in their pay'. Such an increase should be made contingent upon the attainment of prescribed levels of performance. Thus the desire for money which all men were assumed to possess could be directly harnessed to work activity so as to increase performance and efficiency. Employees were assumed to be rational people who made their own sensible decisions about financial gain and loss.

It is through the explicit formulation and use of this second 'law' that Taylor has been particularly influential. The assumption that man works primarily for money and will rationally choose to do that which provides the greatest personal economic gain is the lesson conventionally culled from scientific management. Certainly, the relationship between payment by results and work performance has been sufficiently well illustrated to ensure the use of financial incentive schemes throughout the industrial world. It is only to be regretted that other aspects of Taylor's thinking did not exert an equal influence over the development of industrial psychology. His writing reveals, if only in embryonic form, a concern for issues including those that today have become known as performance appraisal, job analysis, job evaluation, job design, ergonomics, selection and training. His research is also important for its deliberate use of the methodological techniques of control and criterion groups.

Rarely, however, is he credited with these contributions. It is his strong emphasis on man's desire for money, and his contention that management should manipulate pay in order to obtain greater effort from employees, that have survived over the years. Understandably, then, it has become customary to denigrate Taylor's work for its exploitative implications. While his methods did improve the individual's pay they regularly resulted in a proportionately greater benefit for the employer. Moreover, his belief that workmen were basically lazy and should not, for their own good, be allowed to earn too much, has not endeared him to those with less élitist tendencies.

In spite of these features one should not lose sight of the influence exerted by Taylor over our views of human nature. We believe it to be unfortunate, and to a large extent the fault of those who followed and reacted against Taylor, that important aspects of his approach have been virtually ignored. The concept of the 'task idea', foı example, took many years to re-emerge, and his concern for scientifically acceptable methodology influenced even those who disagreed with his conclusions. It should also be noted that economic and technological characteristics have altered since his time. He was working within an expanding economy with a low rate of change. Jobs were differentiated, less interdependent than today, and technological factors closely determined the nature of work. The jobs he studied were relatively unsophisticated, quite unlike many present-day tasks involving monitored decision-making based upon detailed knowledge. This is not to say that Taylor should receive especial praise; but it would be wrong to bury him.

The Hawthorne studies

In contrast with the assumption which emanated from scientific management, that basically man wants only money, the Hawthorne studies promoted a consideration of human relations factors. These studies are of considerable interest in themselves. They have also had a substantial impact upon the course of job attitude research in particular and upon industrial psychology and sociology in general.

The Hawthorne Works were part of the Western Electric Company of Chicago, USA. This was a progressive company for its day, employing around 29,000 people, and paying relatively high wages in addition to providing pension schemes, sickness benefits and recreational facilities. Between 1924 and 1926 a series of studies, later known as the Illumination Experiments, were launched at the Hawthorne Works. These studies reflected the assumptions of their time – efficiency was the overriding concern and the rational individual the object of study. The initial aims were in keeping with prevalent scientific management ideals, in that the researchers intended to measure and control physical features of work in order to increase individual output and efficiency. In three departments, where women employees wound coils, assembled relays and inspected small parts, a number of engineers investigated the relationship between light intensity and work performance.

In the first study the illumination in the workrooms was steadily increased and the effect on production observed. The expectancy was that output would vary systematically with light intensity, but no such simple pattern occurred. In one department production fluctuated randomly relative to illumination. Production in the other two departments did increase, but this increase showed a tenuous and erratic relationship with light intensity. The experimenters next carried out investigations in which two comparable groups of employees were selected for study. The intensity of illumination was kept constant for one group acting as a control for the other. In the latter, lighting levels were gradually increased over time. As predicted, the output of this experimental group increased. But so too did the performance of the control group. With commendable persistence the investigators devised a third series of experiments. Again, the control group illumination was kept constant, but the experimental group received an ever-*decreasing* level of illumination. Once again, however, output rose in both groups, until the experimental group protested that they could no longer see what they were doing. By now the investigators had no option but to abandon their simple hypothesis that on its own light intensity directly affected productivity. Quite clearly other factors were more responsible for the variations in performance.

In 1927 a further set of experiments was conducted in the Hawthorne Works in collaboration with a group of social scientists from the Harvard School of Business Administration under the supervision of Elton Mayo. The account of this study was later written by Roethlisberger and Dickson (1939). The first stage of the inquiry, in the Relay Assembly Test Room, took place over a period of more than two years. Six experienced women employees were selected and transferred to a specially prepared test room. These operatives were engaged in assembling telephone relays, work which was easily measurable and entirely under the control of the individual. At the outset, each employee was told the purpose of the studies, which was to measure the effect of various changes in work conditions upon performance. A first change was the introduction of a group payment scheme. Previously the women had been paid on the performance of about a hundred people carrying out the same kind of work. Under the new scheme the participants in the experiment were paid according to the output of their own, small group. This alteration to piecework arrangements was followed by series of changes which included the introduction of rest pauses of different lengths and at different times during the working day, refreshments, and shorter working hours. In all, ten different combinations of rest pauses and hours worked were tried. Each change in work conditions was discussed with the operatives before being introduced, and communication between experimenters and participants was continuous throughout the investigation. For much of the time an observer was present to record the weather, activities in the test room, and so on. Almost without exception each change in work conditions – for better or for worse – was accompanied by some increase in output.

The penultimate change was the most dramatic. The group was returned to a forty-eight-hour, five-and-a-half-day week with no rest pauses. Output remained high, and the operatives worked much faster than they had under identical conditions near the beginning of the investigations. Finally, they were exposed to a set of working conditions which duplicated those of an earlier experimental period. Overall production reached an all-time high.

The investigators initially found difficulty in interpreting these results. Clearly, the experimental changes could not be used to explain the major finding, that output continually went up. These increases were relatively independent of any specific set of working conditions. So the first conclusion came to be that, at least in this situation, a number of supposedly important factors were really of no demonstrable significance. What, then, accounted for the increased productivity? The change from the large-group to the small-group payment scheme was judged to be of some importance, but the full explanation came to focus upon social factors within the group. Supervision was free and easy, the operatives were able to set their own work pace, and they developed their own norms, practices and values. The removal of the girls from their usual work environment set them apart and intensified the interaction among them. An interest was shown in each individual, and the production record of the group became a source of pride. A sense of cooperation between supervisor and operative was also developed. As a result of these changes in the social milieu, the attitudes of the employees in the experiment became more and more favourable. In other words, an increased involvement in the job was reflected in a steady improvement in production.

The importance of social relationships was further illustrated in two other investigations conducted at the Hawthorne Works. The first of these was a mass interview programme, involving over 21,000 employees, which aimed to discover the nature of attitudes towards work. People were found to have strong views about the physical conditions of their work and about pay, but in practice it was the content and style of their personal relationships which really mattered to them. How their foreman treated them, and how they got along with their colleagues were matters which arose repeatedly throughout the interview programme.

The importance of such issues was further highlighted in the final part of the investigation. This took place in the Bank Wiring Observation Room and was designed to shed more light on what happens within working groups. (Note how far this aim has shifted from the initial objectives of the Illumination Experiments.) Fourteen men were closely studied over a period of six months in 1931 and 1932. Their behaviour and work output was continuously recorded, but no experimental changes in working conditions were introduced. Of the fourteen operatives, nine were employed to wire banks of terminals, three soldered these banks and two worked as inspectors. A fairly complex group payment scheme was employed, and it soon became apparent that the employees did not understand the detailed operation of this scheme although they had a clear enough idea about what they would earn for specified levels of output.

In practice, however, the incentive scheme was not operating as management intended, since the employees did not attempt to maximize their earnings by working harder. Instead the group established its own norms of output. Individuals encouraged each other to keep closely to the agreed production level. If they exceeded this they were expected to record their output as lower than it really was, and the excess would then be recorded in periods of under-production. The social norms of the work-group were clearly having a marked influence on what people did at their work. Taylor's view of rational-economic man seemed to the investigators to be quite inappropriate in this case.

Several other features of the Bank Wiring Observation Room are of interest, and reviews and analyses may be found in Homans (1950), Landsberger (1958), and Mayo (1946). We may here summarize the Hawthorne studies' importance in terms of their developing emphasis on social relationships at work. In retrospect it seems obvious that social factors matter to people in their jobs, but the significance of the studies should be assessed within their historical context. They changed the focus of attention from the physical aspects of the work environment and the incentive value of pay to a consideration of interpersonal relations and communications, group norms and values, participation, supervision, morale and satisfaction. Man was no longer seen as a simple animal driven by a desire for money and at the mercy of his environment. A more complex view had emerged.

Equally importantly, after the initial stages the investigations represented an effort to understand individuals from a standpoint which was less dependent upon the managerial goal of increasing economic efficiency. Good human relations at work themselves became a desirable end, and research and practice turned to an examination of the nature and causes of 'good' relationships. In part, however, the enthusiasm with which some managers and researchers in the 1940s and 1950s grasped this idea was almost certainly due to their assumption that good human relations would themselves lead to more effective operation. For example, it was optimistically assumed that conflict between management and workers could be cut out altogether by better communication and the establishment of friendly work-groups.

Mayo's theory was of undoubted importance, but in its development and subsequent interpretation it came to overemphasize social factors and to place too little stress on other aspects of work. Commentators soon inferred from the Hawthorne studies that pay was of no importance at all; this interpretation should be seen as much in terms of a reaction to scientific management as a statement of the facts evidenced in the Hawthorne research.

Maslow's theory of human nature

A third influence upon job attitude research is to be found in the work of Maslow (1943, 1968, 1970, 1973). This differs in two main ways from the approaches already described in this chapter. Firstly, his theory of human nature was not developed specifically as an attempt to understand people at work. Maslow was more a clinical, humanistic psychologist than one concerned with industrial and other organizations. As such his work is broader in scope, being concerned with motivation in life more generally; we have already mentioned some of his views on psychological growth (page 17). Secondly, his theory is not only an attempt to identify people's wants; it goes beyond identification to specify the relationships between them in terms of their hierarchical organization.

Maslow postulated that man has five classes of 'basic needs'. The first is a physiological need, a desire for food, water and other prerequisites of life. The second, a safety need, involves a wish for security and the avoidance of physical danger. The third class – social needs – involves a desire for affection and friendship. The fourth is a need for esteem, a desire for a high evaluation of oneself, for self-respect. The final need is for 'self-actualization'. This is the most original aspect of his theory and at the same time the concept most difficult to define.

Maslow distinguishes between 'becoming' and 'being'. We are all the time in the process of moving towards our full potential, towards the actualization of what we might be. This process of movement is one of 'becoming', and we are closer on some occasions than others to 'being' our true selves. Maslow writes of self-actualization as both a process and as a momentary experience of being. Some quotations from his later works will help to give the flavour of his approach.

> We may define [self-actualization] as an episode, or a spurt in which the powers of the person come together in a particularly efficient and intensely enjoyable way, and in which he is more integrated and less split, more open for experience, more idiosyncratic, more perfectly expressive or spontaneous, or fully functioning, more creative, more humorous, more ego-transcending, more independent of his lower needs, etc. He becomes in these episodes more truly himself, more perfectly actualizing his potentialities, closer to the core of his Being, more fully human [1968, p. 97].
>
> Self-actualization is a relatively achieved 'state of affairs' in a few people. In most people, however, it is rather a hope, a yearning, a drive, a 'something' wished for but not yet achieved, showing itself clinically as drive towards health, integration, growth etc. [1968, p. 160].
>
> Self-actualization means experiencing fully, vividly, selflessly, with ull concentration and total absorption . . . Self-actualization is an

ongoing process; it means making each of the many single choices about whether to lie or be honest, whether to steal or not to steal at a particular point, and it means to make each of these choices as a growth choice . . . Looking within oneself for many of the answers implies taking responsibility. That is in itself a great step towards actualization . . . Self-actualization is not only an end state but also the process of actualizing one's potentialities at any time, in any amount. It is, for example, a matter of becoming smarter by studying if one is an intelligent person . . . Self-actualization means working to do well the thing that one wants to do . . . Put all these points together, and we see that self-actualization is not a matter of one great moment. It is not true that on Thursday at four o'clock the trumpet blows and one steps into the pantheon forever and altogether. Self-actualization is a matter of degree, of little accessions accumulated one by one [1973, p. 52].

In Maslow's theory, then, the need to self-actualize is a particularly important one. He argues that the five kinds of basic needs form a hierarchy, from self-actualization at the top, through esteem, social and safety needs to physiological needs. The lower-order needs are seen as prepotent: they are personally most significant until they are satisfied to some acceptable degree, and only then do the higher needs gradually come into play. The higher needs are extremely important, but not until the others are satisfied. Conversely the lower needs can monopolize consciousness and behaviour when they have not been met. Man does not live by bread alone, but when he has no bread his active wants are exclusively to do with food.

These thoughts have been incorporated into the mainstream of occupational and organizational psychology by the recognition that employment in most industrialized societies caters quite well for lower-level needs. The wants which the theory predicts to be important to people are the higher-level ones to do with esteem and actualization. So what has work to offer here? For manual workers in most jobs it offers very little indeed. Can we then design jobs so that people's work engages their higher-level needs? This clearly presents difficult technological and financial problems.

Maslow's theory can be discussed on several levels. The conclusion of the last paragraph suggests that managers and employers might reject it on practical grounds, and certainly many so do. Yet we believe that a large number of people in professional and managerial jobs know for themselves what Maslow is driving at. His writings are florid and idealistic, but his notion of self-actualization strikes home to many. Management theorists like Argyris (1964), Likert (1961) and McGregor (1960) have built their prescriptions around the idea, and many managers are caught between conflicting forces: they want to accept the notion of self-actualization at work for themselves, but practical reasons make it difficult for them to accept it for their manual employees. This point will recur throughout the book.

A second level of criticism of Maslow's theory is, however, possible. This concerns his identification of separate needs which are ordered hierarchically. Several research programmes have employed separate measures (e.g. Porter 1961, 1962, 1963; Porter and Lawler, 1968) but there is ample evidence of overlap between the supposedly discrete want-systems (e.g. Payne 1970; Schneider and Alderfer, 1973). Studies of the hierarchical nature of these systems are difficult because they require a shift beyond merely cross-sectional investigations; the essence of Maslow's proposals is that the prepotency of need systems changes with time, so that longitudinal research is essential. A start in this direction has been made by Alderfer (1973).

A third level of criticism is in terms of the broad-ranging, sometimes vague and sometimes inconsistent nature of Maslow's theorizing. Such criticism is probably valid, but also embodies Maslow's strength in the context of this chapter. His theme is the complex nature of motivation, and the positive forward-looking aspects of our most important wants: a large step from the tenets of scientific management.

Herzberg's two-factor theory

A related theory which from its inception has been aimed specifically at the organization of work is that of Herzberg *et al.* (1959). During the late 1960s this theory generated more research investigations than any other in the field of job attitudes. Outside academic circles it was also very influential, partly because of Herzberg's persuasive skill as a consultant and conference participant.

The central proposition of the two-factor theory is that the determinants of job satisfaction are qualitatively different from the determinants of job dissatisfaction. When it was first proposed, as a result of a review of the job attitude literature, Herzberg expressed it this way:

> The one dramatic finding that emerged was the fact that there was a difference in the primacy of factors, depending upon whether the investigator was looking for things the worker liked about his job, or things he disliked. The concept that there were some factors that were 'satisfiers' and others that were 'dissatisfiers' was suggested by this finding. From it was derived one of the basic hypotheses of our own study [1959, p. 7].

The results of this initial investigation into the views of engineers and accountants, who were asked to describe the causes of their satisfactions and dissatisfactions at work, gave support for the theory; and subsequent studies of the same type yielded broadly consistent results. Five factors stood out as determinants of job satisfaction: achievement, advancement, recognition, responsibility and the work itself. These Herzberg labelled 'motivators', and he argued that they were factors intrinsic to the performance of work itself. In constrast, the factors of company policy and administration, supervision, interpersonal relations and work conditions were strongly related to job dissatisfaction, but apparently unimportant as determinants of satisfaction. This latter set of factors Herzberg called 'hygiene factors', on the medical analogy that without them we are unhealthy, yet increasing them beyond an acceptable level does not make us positively more healthy. Herzberg argued that hygiene factors are extrinsic to the performance of work, being aspects of the work environment rather than of the work itself. Thus a dichotomy is proposed where factors of one kind (intrinsic to the job) promote job satisfaction and factors of a different nature (extrinsic to the job) determine job dissatisfaction. This view is in conflict with the traditional idea that any job factor may cause satisfaction or dissatisfaction depending upon the degree to which it is present or absent.

Herzberg went on to interpret these findings as suggesting that man has two separate and distinct sets of needs – those concerned with the avoidance of pain which are serviced by hygiene factors, and those towards self-actualization reflected in motivators: '. . . the human animal has two categories of needs. One stems from his animal disposition . . . it is centred on the avoidance of loss of life, hunger, pain, sexual deprivation and other primary drives . . . The other segment of man's nature is [a] . . . compelling urge to realize his own potentiality by continuous psychological growth' (Herzberg, 1966, p. 56). The parallel between the hygiene-motivator dichotomy and Maslow's distinction between low-level 'deficit' motives (physiological and safety needs) and higher-level 'growth' motives (self-actualization and esteem) is marked.

The two-factor theory has given rise to considerable controversy. Whereas numerous studies, typically using methodologies similar to that originally used by Herzberg, have provided support for his distinction, equally many investigations, usually adopting different methodologies, have not. The consensus of opinion which has emerged is that the two-factor theory does not stand up to the empirical test. However, even in its failure it has added another important dimension to job attitude research. Almost all of the studies which fail to support Herzberg's theory do so because intrinsic factors (the motivators) are found to be determinants not only of job satisfaction but also of job dissatisfaction (Wall and Stephenson, 1970). In other words, feelings about achievement, responsibility and recognition are repeatedly emphasized as important to job attitudes: these factors which had previously been neglected are now seen as central to the notion of psychological well-being.

The particular significance of the two-factor theory is not simply in the dimensions it emphasizes, but more in the fact that it is sufficiently explicit in formulation to encourage empirical investigation and practical application. Maslow's theory stressed the importance of similar factors, but did not lend itself to empirical test. Herzberg is responsible, both in academic research and in management practice, for giving impetus to a consideration of the positive aspects of well-being. His views on psychological growth (see pages 15 to 17) may have sounded idealistic and utopian to the practical manager, but he has proved well able to convince many sceptical industrialists to try out his recommendations in the field of job design (see page 127). And to the academic he presented a theory which was both controversial and testable.

Conclusions

We have briefly described some of the more important theoretical influences upon both job attitude research and management practices. In doing this we have taken the view that each of the approaches considered was an element in an ever-broadening view of human nature as it relates to the work environment. We should emphasize, however, that each theory did not evolve in a vacuum; rather it was a development from the inadequacy of its predecessors. Thus the influence of the Hawthorne studies may be attributed to the fact that they provided a plausible alternative to the clearly restricted views of Taylor as well as to their emphasis on social factors. Maslow's theory has been influential because the notion that man wanted only money or social contact was obviously too simple. Finally, the influence of Herzberg's work is a result of its applicability for research and management practice, an applicability lacking in Maslow's more general formulation.

Following this historical summary we may now turn to look at some of the major aspects of work which influence psychological well-being. These will be examined in roughly the sequence followed in the present chapter. So we begin with pay.

3 Systems and levels of pay

Despite the emphasis placed upon pay in early studies of what people want from work, more recent theorists have tended to give only limited attention to financial questions. In part this reflects the growing concentration on positive aspects of well-being, which we have traced in the previous two chapters, and in part it represents the continuing reaction against the more manipulative features of scientific management.

Yet the evidence for the central role of wages in people's thought and action has never been countermanded. Studies reviewed by Lawler (1971, p. 218) are consistent in their conclusion that pay is regularly the job aspect with which the greatest number of employees express dissatisfaction. This is reflected in everyday experience, where industrial disputes and strikes regularly have as their immediate cause a disagreement over pay; this disagreement often spreads well beyond the initial question of money. People choose jobs and move from one to another for obviously financial reasons. Even the Hawthorne studies (see page 27) pointed frequently to economic issues. The initial increases in output in the Relay Assembly Test Room were clearly attributed in part by the investigators to the operation of a revised payment-by-results scheme, and work performance in the Bank Wiring Observation Room was also linked to the particular payment scheme employed there. Especially salient were results of the interview programme in the same study. We have already noted how questions of social relationships were repeatedly raised, but in practice the topic most often introduced by employees was that of pay (Mayo, 1946, p. 90). Despite these observations, many commentators have mistakenly seen the Hawthorne results as demonstrating the minor significance of money.

Such a conclusion has never made much sense to workers or managers, and it is gratifying to see as one more sign of psychology's increasing relevance to people at work a resurgence of interest in pay. In this chapter we shall examine some of the studies and theories which have recently appeared. As with other topics covered in this book our emphasis is upon what people want, and our central question here concerns the amount of pay that they regard as appropriate for a particular job. In an absolute sense people may well want huge sums of money, but in a relative sense their practical concern is with a fair return for their work in the context of the amounts received by other people. We shall examine this concern later in the chapter; the importance of pay and types of payment system will first be considered.

The reported importance of pay

Granting that pay is to most people a central aspect of work, investigators have often been tempted to be more specific: *how* central is pay? *how much* does it matter to people? Answers to these questions naturally require comparison with other aspects of work: is pay more important than, say, social companionship? In this way there have emerged studies in which employees make paired-comparison or rank-order judgements of importance of different aspects of their work.

Few of these studies should be taken very seriously. They are beset with methodological problems, arising primarily from the question which judges are asked. The answer to the question, 'Is pay more important to you than social companionship?' depends crucially upon the meaning given to 'important'. Do you judge importance in your present job, in an ideal job, in general, at a time of changing jobs; and are your judgements about the feelings you would experience if pay were taken away, if it were increased, stayed the same, or what? It is customary to leave the instructions relatively unspecific.

Whatever the basis on which judgements are made, the reported importance of pay naturally varies according to individual circumstances at the time a judgement is made. In an insecure job you may trouble more over security than pay.

With a young family to support you may feel that pay matters above all other job features. In a job that pays generously other components of your work become salient. Cultural factors also affect how strongly people feel about their pay: Goldthorpe *et al.* (1968) illustrated how groups of workers may combine an 'instrumental' orientation to their jobs (being concerned primarily to use work to gain money for out-of-work satisfaction) with a geographical mobility (seeking work which pays well). On the other hand, there are many settled communities where concerns for stability, tradition and friendships override feelings that money is worth troubling too much about.

It is extremely difficult to draw general conclusions from reported importance studies for another reason. Each study has used its own instructions and has employed different items to be judged. The relative importance of pay in a study of only four job aspects is inappropriately combined with its rank order in a study of twenty job aspects. In the latter case the picture is additionally confused since pay may well appear in different guises (fringe benefits, pension schemes and so on, in addition to wages or salaries). A statement about the overall importance of pay in relation to other aspects of work is thus of limited validity.

Lawler has reviewed studies in this area, and his conclusion is worth quoting. 'Most of the research is fragmented, non-cumulative, and poorly designed. Most of the studies that have tried to determine how important pay is represent a great expenditure of effort that contributes virtually nothing to our understanding' (1971, p. 59). Taking their results at face value, however, he shows that the average importance ranking of pay is about third. We would stress the economic context of any study, pointing out that the research summarized by Lawler spans forty very different years. The early 1970s have seen a period of rapid inflation, quite different from the economic climate in, say, the 1930s. During a time of inflation when newspapers, union meetings and workingmen's clubs are heavy with talk of 30 per cent wage rises it is obvious that pay takes on a special significance.

The concern throughout this book with what people want from their work is another way of looking at these studies of reported importance. It is helpful to distinguish between 'episodic wants' and 'dispositional wants' (see page 168). An episodic want is a want-in-context ('How much pay do you want now for your present job?') whereas a dispositional want is a longer-term, generalized one. In studying the relative importance of pay or any other goal-object we need to study the strength of *dispositional* wants. In practice the measures have often been of an episodic nature, and it is clear that when an episodic want is relatively satisfied it declines in contemporary importance (cf. Lawler and Porter, 1963; see also the discussion of a hierarchy of needs in Chapter 2). The results of studies in this area have often been too much a reflection of current satisfaction and not sufficiently an index of dispositional wants or more general value-orientations.

The intention behind studies of reported importance might be better served by asking questions which more clearly deal with generalized wants, irrespective of a person's current job situation. In so doing we would come closer to studies of personality-linked motivational systems: some people characteristically rate achievement more highly than companionship, others rate financial reward more highly than either. In such an area it is more sensible to stress the differences between people or groups of people than to ask for an overall comparison among the strengths of achievement, affiliation and money motives for the population as a whole.

With respect to people's concern for pay, Lawler's (1971) review suggests that sex differences are of particular importance. Research and common knowledge agree that men tend to feel more strongly about pay than do women. Such a difference may well partly arise from discrepances in domestic responsibilities, although Lawler claims that it emerges even with women employees who are heads of households (1971, p. 47). Many occupations in the United Kingdom have traditionally paid less to women even when they carry out the same work as men, although legislation for equal pay is gradually having an impact on this situation.

Strength of feeling about pay is also known to decline with age. Such an effect is partly due to increasing earnings with age but also to a change in values and responsibilities and a growing concern for security as people grow older. Similarly, economic influences (arising from the size of your family, for example) are important irrespective of age, as are cultural differences arising from the operation of social pressures on group members' goals.

In summary, studies of the reported importance of job features should be treated with caution. It is evident almost to the point of tautology that pay is central to work, and people's feelings and behaviour reflect this. Furthermore, many other features of work are clearly less central. Not surprisingly there are differences between people in their strength of feeling about pay, and progress in this area is likely to require a concentration upon dispositional rather than episodic wants.

Systems of payment

We turn now to an examination of what kind of payment system people prefer. This question is of obvious practical importance, and helpful discussions have been provided by Lawler (1971), Lupton (1972), Marriott (1957), North and Buckingham (1969), Shimmin (1959) and others. Psychologists' research into pay has largely been at an abstract, general level, so that investigators have often been reluctant to maintain close contact with complex ongoing situations. If such research is to be really valuable to the practitioner or indeed to the psychologist, the latter has to acquire a more detailed understanding than he usually does of the 'nuts and bolts' of the payment procedure and industrial relations climate of the organization in which he is working.

These 'nuts and bolts' may be introduced by a look at the major methods of payment. The simplest procedure is usually referred to as 'timework'. People paid on timework receive the same wages per hour (or per week, month or year) irrespective of how hard or successfully they work during that time. In graphical terms timework payment is as shown in Figure 3.1. This makes it obvious that the major issue to be settled when agreeing a timework system is the level of payment itself, since this remains constant over conditions. The payment level is usually subject to negotiation and is often referred to as the 'job value' of the work in question. In practice there may be a scale of payments based on the job value to allow for annual increments or merit rises; these are more customary in white-collar than in blue-collar jobs. (Inquiring minds might be tempted to ask why.)

Figure 3.1 Payment by time

'Payment by results' (or 'piecework') schemes are also based upon a job value (how much the job is worth) but different sums are paid according to how hard or successfully an employee works. A huge variety of payment-by-results schemes have been tried out over the years, but the two main types are as in Figure 3.2. The left-hand diagram there illustrates a 'straight piecework' scheme. In this there is a direct association between amount produced and amount earned. The slope of the line (how steep or flat it is) is determined by two calculations – job value and standard performance (J.V. and S.P. in the figure). Standard performance is the amount which should be produced under normal piecework conditions (a figure usually determined through work measurement procedures), and job value is (as before) the amount the job is agreed to be worth.

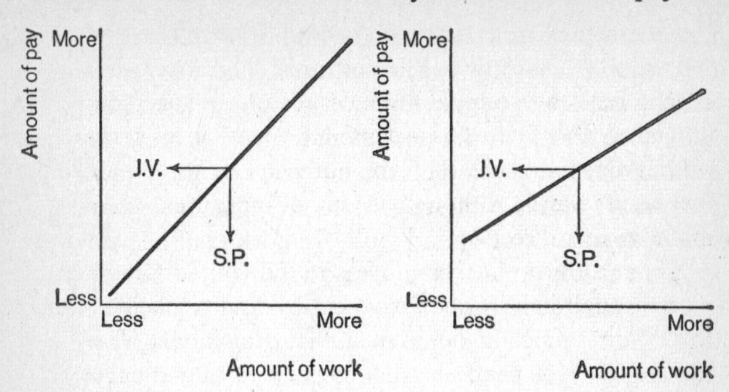

Figure 3.2 Payment by results

The right-hand diagram in Figure 3.2. illustrates a 'bonus scheme' where the so-called incentive element is smaller. Once again the establishment of such a scheme depends upon the determination of job value and standard performance, but the scheme is constructed so that the amount of pay received varies less markedly with changes in output. If the amount of work done is below standard performance (perhaps when an employee is tired or unwell, or when only limited work is available) he gains relative to the 'steeper' system in the left-hand diagram. But if he can easily exceed standard performance (because of additional effort or perhaps because the rate is a 'loose' one) he is at a disadvantage relative to straight piecework.

Opinions differ from time to time and from place to place about the desirability of steep or flat payment-by-results schemes. The most common view in the United Kingdom at present (unions' and employers') appears to be that a bonus element of between 25 per cent and 35 per cent of total earnings is about right. This protects workers in difficult times, but still provides a sufficient opportunity for individuals to increase their pay by extra effort and skill.

Nevertheless there is a trend in some industries to introduce a third type of payment. This combines the constant payment of timework with the standard performance and higher job values attached to piecework. Under 'measured daywork' a target is agreed, and if it is met the employees receive the higher job value payment which is customary for the pieceworker. If it is not, they receive lower wages unless machine breakdowns or other factors have caused this to happen. Increases in output beyond the target are not usually accompanied by increased wages, although in some industries there is a move in this direction.

About a third of all employees in the United Kingdom are paid through some form of payment-by-results scheme, though this figure is much higher in manufacturing industries where it can approach 50 per cent About 9 per cent of manual workers are paid on measured daywork, although industries such as motor manufacturing and coal-mining employ it much more extensively (Office of Manpower Economics, 1973). Some timeworkers receive a variable payment through 'lieu rates' or 'factory efficiency bonuses'. These are additional wages paid in lieu of the pieceworkers' bonus to those members of the work-force whose jobs are not open to work measurement.

Individual and group schemes

The simplest forms of payment-by-results schemes are those in which an individual employee's income is determined by the amount he himself produces. A machine operator might receive wages in proportion to the output from his machine, or a salesman might be paid commission for his sales. In many cases however a necessary interdependence between workers means that no single individual is alone responsible for the work. In these cases a group payment-by-results scheme may be instituted, such that each person's pay is determined by the output of the group as a whole. Within such a scheme there may be different job values so that a leading hand, for example, may receive more than his colleagues.

Individual piecework naturally brings problems in complex production situations where a single worker is increasingly dependent upon other people. On smooth-running days all may be well, but when materials are not available from other workers, when the quality of the part-finished product reaching him is uncertain, or when his machine is temporarily out of order, attribution of responsibility and calculation of special allowances can be time-consuming and may give rise to disputes. Individual piecework may also cause friction in that separate employees compete for the jobs which pay more generously. Whyte (1955), Lupton (1963) and others have provided interesting illustrations of this. Babchuk and Goode's (1951) account of store salesmen on individual piecework described how ancillary work like stock-checking and labelling was avoided as employees competed for customers; eventually an informal pooling of sales was agreed.

Some major companies in Holland, Denmark and elsewhere have reported success with what is in effect a group measured daywork system. Production employees agree an output target for, say, a three-month period. Their earnings during this period are paid at target level and the group has some autonomy in choosing its methods and pace of work. The psychological principles behind this approach and some organizational implications are considered in Chapter 6.

Some effects of payment by results

In examining people's reactions to particular payment schemes the effects of these schemes naturally require consideration. One obvious effect of introducing a payment-by-results scheme is likely to be an increase in output. In part this may arise from other organizational changes made simultaneously, but there is no doubt that it does generally occur. Indeed, conventional work-study and industrial relations practices take it for granted that payment for standard performance should be higher than timework payment, because that standard performance is itself higher than the performance expected of timeworkers.

In organizational terms an extensive payment-by-results programme can create problems and interpersonal frictions quite unheard of in timework factories. These arise primarily from the increase in bargaining which is required, since both job value and standard performance now have to be negotiated. In a large production department making batches of different items there may be more than 150 different rates on the books at any one time. A typical week might see the introduction of two new rates. These will probably be variants of jobs already being worked, but they will nevertheless require attention from foremen, managers, worker representatives and work-study engineers.

A major focus of this attention will be a new rate's comparability with earlier ones, and here the distinction between 'tight' and 'loose' rates becomes important. In most departments some piecework jobs allow higher earnings than others. These 'loose' rates may arise through errors by management, through subsequent increases in workers' skill, changes in materials or better equipment. Not unnaturally, also, the employees who are subject to time study or other forms of work measurement associated with a new rate will emphasize during the studies how difficult the job is, and their difficulties may well extend through the 'trial period' that the new rate may be subject to. In these ways there is a continuing emphasis upon the looseness or tightness of rates: workers strive for loose rates and use them as comparisons when new schemes are proposed.

One wide-ranging set of consequences of payment by results is thus concerned with increased friction and argument. The situation is one of continual introduction of change where the financial stakes are high for both management and workers. In attitudinal terms the schemes may lead to an emphasis on money beyond that desired by both of the sides involved. An atmosphere of mutual mistrust is likely to develop, and management may generally attempt to tighten its control on quality, discipline and other day-to-day features of the workplace. These attempts will involve supervisory checks on what people are doing, and often require an elaborate system of paper-work and book-keeping. An us-and-them perspective which emphasizes conflicts and minimizes collaboration can in these ways easily arise from, but extend much beyond, disputes over money.

Several of these points are captured in the following account by a manual worker in a small factory. The new piecework scheme was apparently a generous one.

Only, in practice it didn't work out like that. In the first place, the 'task definition' wasn't too good. Arguments arose later as to whether rejects counted, who did the rectification, what allowance was made for faulty or badly-fitting material, etc. Pieceworkers were dependent on 'day-rate' workers for the bringing of material and the removing of the finished product; and when, later, the number of these day-rate workers was reduced, some of these tasks fell very gradually on the shoulders of the pieceworkers. Secondly, there were fierce arguments about the accuracy of the timing . . . Sometimes you could get it revised, by a combination of bluff and bluster; sweet reason got you nowhere. So we ended up with some rates that were quite good – one assembly line was known as 'The Golden Mile' – and many that were not so good. On these, not only did the piecework fail to live up to the rosy promises of the management; you sometimes had to cut corners to break even [Fraser, 1969, p. 292].

Payment systems are also seen by some as features of a more general political struggle within society. A union official writes:

While [union] leadership counts for a lot, the method of payment in a factory has an important bearing on the organization and militancy of the workers inside it, for the method can help to mould the basis of activity. At our plant we work straight piecework . . . It has certain advantages: it is direct, it can lead to higher earnings, and it gives the workers a measure of control over their production. The continual battle over rates makes the workers very militant, for when the rate-fixer comes out to argue with you, you're immediately faced with the basic element of the class struggle: exploitation, potential or actual [Fraser, 1969, pp. 112–13].

Furthermore, a small minority of trade unionists see incentive schemes as unacceptable attempts by management to weaken the solidarity of a work-force. They prefer to negotiate single payments for all employees within a grade, arguing that piecework systems introduce undesirable competition between individual workers. A proposed incentive scheme was rejected by the National Union of Mineworkers in 1974; delegates from South Wales maintained that its divisiveness would involve 'a betrayal of membership and the destruction of the union'. Such views are not widely held (we recorded on page 46 how almost half the total employees in manufacturing industry are paid through payment-by-results schemes), but their influence can be considerable in times of dispute.

Restriction of output

As noted above, when new jobs are introduced workers may well emphasize their difficulty by turning out only a limited quantity of work. This should cause no surprise. But when payment-by-results schemes have been agreed and are in operation the expectation might be that individuals will try to produce as much as possible so that their take-home pay can be increased. In practice it is quite usual for an informal work-group quota or norm to be set, and for people to restrict their output to this quota.

In terms of immediate cash such restriction makes little sense, but there are several other justifications for it. Avoidance of fatigue, fear of rate-cutting, the need to protect slower workers, and a desire to avoid too much competition between workers are among the reasons typically given. Other motives derive from the control which workers gain over their own target and pace of work and from their ability to avoid being obviously manipulated by management. Individuals may of course reach their own decision about a reasonable quota in isolation from others, but in practice there is almost always a strong group feeling behind the establishment and maintenance of these norms. Their basis in group relationships will be further examined in Chapter 4.

Restriction of output has been discussed by Hickson (1961), Lupton (1963), Whyte (1955), Zaleznik, Christensen and Roethlisberger (1958) and many others. Roy (1952) cites cases where the quota for an eight-hour shift was usually achieved in six hours, allowing two hours' pleasant association with colleagues. In many plants 'underbooking' of output is usual, so that work produced but not claimed for can be booked on later occasions when output might be lower (e.g. Millward, 1972). Parenthetically it should be noted that several commentators have attributed the discovery of quota restriction to the Hawthorne investigators, who examined its operation in the Bank Wiring Observation Room (see page 31). In practice the issue was of interest well before that time; Myers (1920) devotes a whole chapter to it and presents many detailed illustrations.

The comprehensibility of payment systems

Myers also noted how workers' attitudes to their payment system were often coloured by its unintelligibility (1920, p. 144), and this characteristic of payment schemes is still extremely common. In Millward's study

> the system of calculating the production bonus . . . was entirely unknown to the operators, supervisors and shop stewards in the assembly department. Some of them had a vague idea that it was related to the piecework bonus for the whole department; others thought that it depended upon 'what went out the door', i.e. the amount of finished work that left the factory. None of them knew that it was paid as a percentage of their piecework basic rate . . . Having no clear idea of what it was for or how it was calculated the operators, not surprisingly, saw themselves as powerless to influence the production bonus. They were pleased when it went up and annoyed when it went down [1972, p. 356].

A helpful distinction is drawn by Shimmin (1959) between 'functional' and 'formal' understanding. Work-groups usually have a fairly good functional understanding of their payment arrangements: they can anticipate the earnings levels which are in practice associated with different levels of output. The formal structure of the scheme, often with accretions of special payments, allowances and bonuses for particular circumstances, is much less often comprehended by the average production worker.

Job evaluation

The process which establishes the worth of jobs is usually termed 'job evaluation'. Several different job evaluation schemes are available, but these all share a process of comparative judgement. Jobs within a department or factory are ranked, compared in twos, or each rated in terms of certain features. These features might include degree of physical effort, working conditions, length of learning period, level of responsibility and so on. It is usual for a small number of 'benchmark jobs' to be studied with special care so that once their placement is fixed other jobs can be more easily located.

The primary aim of job evaluation is to produce a small series of grades which fairly reflect the differing worths of jobs. The sums of money attached to this grade structure are decided through a separate process, so that the final job values are a product of the two separate operations. Both managers and trade unions seem to agree in principle that job evaluation is desirable, but in practice there are of course snags. Over the years most departments have acquired a payment structure which is in places unbalanced, so that certain operatives are overpaid in relation to others. To wipe the slate clean and to write in a newly evaluated structure would almost certainly mean that the jobs performed by these individuals should carry a reduced wage. It is strongly believed, however, that reductions in wages are not permissible: one must always bargain up, never down. Various forms of 'protected earnings' for the present incumbents are used, but nevertheless the practical difficulties of renewing a wages structure in its entirety are considerable.

Another traditional attitude which still holds sway in some industries is a profound dislike for any activity to do with work study; such an attitude naturally precludes the development of any sophisticated payment-by-results or job evaluation schemes. The techniques evolved by work-study engineers have their origin in the early scientific management movement, and as this movement became hated for its excesses of repression during the 1920s a lingering distrust is not surprising. Most of the larger trade unions in the United Kingdom have, however, now accepted the use of work study, though they naturally wish to monitor its application and to build appropriate safeguards into their agreements.

Profit-sharing

In addition to individual or group payment-by-results schemes some companies have instituted arrangements whereby employees receive as a proportion of their income a component based on the profits of the organization as a whole. This proportion is usually very small and its relationship to a single operative's effort is necessarily tenuous. Practical difficulties are to be anticipated in unprofitable periods, and very many government or non-profit organizations are of course excluded. For senior managers in entrepreneurial organizations the potential performance–reward link is sometimes clear and attitudes to profit-sharing are often positive, but the average industrial worker appears to react more negatively. Trade union policy is often to prefer larger all-round increases in times of particularly good profits, and more traditional unionists oppose the general principle of sharing on the grounds that management is covertly attempting to lead the working class down the paths of capitalism.

In recent years there has been discussion among politicians about ways of increasing employee involvement in their organizations. One suggestion has centred upon profit-distribution through shareholdings, and this type of suggestion may increase interest in the possibilities of profit-sharing. But at the moment most workers appear to have little interest in this type of payment.

The Scanlon plan

There have however been attempts to apply schemes which include profit sharing as merely one component of a broad managerial philosophy. The best known of these is the Scanlon plan, named after Joseph Scanlon – an American steelworkers' union official whose basic training was as a cost accountant. The proposals which later came together to form the 'plan' were first tried out in the late 1930s, and they have been popular in varying degrees since then. (Several papers reprinted by Lupton, 1972, detail these developments; see also Lawler, 1971; Schultz and McKersie, 1973.)

In terms of payment the Scanlon plan operates a collective bonus based on an overall assessment of labour costs. The usual procedure is for unions and management to agree on a 'normal' labour cost for the factory and then on ways to give employees the benefits of any savings beyond that 'normal' level. The plan incorporates a suggestion scheme, whereby employees are invited to recommend improvements in working procedures and conditions. This is typically linked with a wider emphasis on participative styles of management, in that supervisors are encouraged to seek out and respond positively to subordinates' opinions about their work. Attempts are made to harness group enthusiasm, so that for instance individuals putting forward suggestions are not themselves rewarded for them: the gain is the group's. Included in the plan is a network of committees so that proposals and developments can be systematically examined and acted upon.

The principles of the Scanlon plan are attractive to many observers, but others point out the practical difficulties. The measurement of labour-cost savings is often difficult, and agreement on how to apportion these savings to employees or to the company is not always achieved. Application of the plan to the whole of a large organization is often seen as too risky, yet its introduction within one small section can yield problems of interdepartmental comparability. The usual problems of understanding have also to be faced: one company's formula for each employee's share is

$$I = 0{\cdot}55\{\Sigma[(W+S+Md+Mi)P]+CS-[Wa+Ma]\}!$$

In addition, the savings on labour costs may temporarily deviate from overall company performance, so that earnings can occasionally go up as the company is running into the red and vice versa. Finally, there is no strong trade union enthusiasm for general application of this kind of plan.

Within the context of United Kingdom industrial relations in the late 1970s it seems probable that variants of the Scanlon plan will emerge as tailor-made pay and productivity deals. The philosophy behind both approaches is one of 'integrative bargaining' where workers and management come together to examine possible joint problem-solving and wage-system developments (McKersie and Hunter, 1973; Walton and McKersie, 1965, Warr, 1973a). The specific content of these developments will sometimes resemble the Scanlon components, but more often it will mainly be the ideology which is similar.

Three-tier payment systems

Many of the aspects of pay schemes noted so far can be brought together into a 'three-tier' system. For manual workers the first component of their pay will be a basic wage attached to the agreed value of their job. The second component might be a variable one arising out of an individual or group payment-by-results scheme, and the third tier would be a more general share-of-prosperity element based upon plant profitability, efficiency or added-value (North and Buckingham, 1969). In terms of a pay packet these three elements might contribute about 70, 25 and 5 per cent respectively.

Informal observations suggest that such a scheme could be very popular. It is of course difficult to obtain adequate evidence on a large scale about workers' opinions, since a final judgement depends on the precise details involved: attitude surveys about imprecise and hypothetical schemes have little to recommend them. But is a three-tier system appropriate for managerial and white-collar employees? We have already observed how profit-sharing appears to be of greater interest among these groups, so that the third tier should present no problems of acceptability. Neither should the first tier; but how far can the second component (personal payment by results) be tied to individual or group performance? Lawler has argued for a greater use of performance-linked salary schemes for managers, though he does conclude that these might be more acceptable in the USA than in Europe (1971, p. 162). Mahoney's (1964) study suggests that even in the USA the proportion of their salary which managers would like in the form of performance-reward is less than 10 per cent.

The basic problem is the accurate measurement of performance. Few managers can be evaluated by a single objective yardstick, and initial optimism that techniques of 'management-by-objectives' (e.g. Humble, 1968, 1970; Mali, 1972) might provide the vital index of effectiveness has waned in many quarters. Some form of judgement by superiors appears necessary, but the management-appraisal schemes in operation in most companies are relatively crude and unreliable. At present there is often little point in increasing the sophistication of formal schemes since the detailed judgements they elicit are rarely used in practice. It is largely the informal evaluation system which produces decisions about promotions, transfers and so on; the formal appraisal procedures support these few changes but are for most managers elaborately redundant. However, if a company chose to introduce a second payment tier for managers, based upon their performance, its appraisal scheme would have to be sufficiently rigorous to gain general confidence.

This is possible (e.g. Warr, 1971a, p. 212) but in the current climate of opinion is rarely seen as worthwhile. A three-tier system for white-collar employees will therefore have to differ from that advocated for manual workers. In practice the second tier is likely to be in terms of annual increments within a pre-determined scale. Many salaried jobs are paid through an incremental scale around a basic job value. The increments assume that greater experience is associated with higher efficiency, which itself should be rewarded; they also represent an equitable recompense for increased service and to some extent for age and loyalty.

Pay secrecy

Another aspect of pay systems is whether the sums received by each individual are made public or kept secret. In most groups of manual workers knowledge about any individual's gross pay is in principle usually obtainable by the others. His grade or job value is typically made public, and functional understanding of a payment-by-results scheme is often adequate for making reasonable guesses about his variable pay. Furthermore, comparison of wage slips and open discussion of individual amounts is quite common.

Among non-manual workers the conventions appear to be different. People paid on publicly announced incremental scales are often aware only of approximate placements of their colleagues, though developing trade unionism amongst these groups may reduce the conventional reticence. In managerial settings the salary scale is often unknown except to a small number of senior people. Managers themselves may want publication of the scales as a whole but most prefer individual salaries to be kept secret. The reasons for this preference deserve closer investigation, but some implications of the practice have already received empirical study. Opsahl and Dunnette (1966) quote research suggesting that managers overestimate the pay of their subordinates and peers but underestimate that of their superiors. Lawler (1971) has been particularly interested in the effects of pay secrecy upon managerial motivation. He concludes that 'open' schemes would increase motivation, but only in organizations where pay and performance are linked (see also Porter and Lawler, 1968).

Studying pay preferences

A general comment should be made at this point about the need for closer investigation of employees preference for particular *types* of payment system. How many organizations have examined attitudes to the three-tier possibility outlined above? How many have thought hard about the secrecy issue? Nealey (1963) has illustrated a useful procedure for studying how employees would prefer to divide up a specified increase in wages. Granting that an increase of a certain amount is appropriate, it is sometimes wise to examine recipients' comparative judgements of how this should be paid. Nealey's research was in the USA, and his alternatives (pension increase, all-round rise, life insurance, additional holidays, etc.) are not all relevant elsewhere. However, his approach is transferable and the differences in choice he reported according to age, family responsibilities, income level and so on are likely to be found quite widely.

Levels of payment

The emphasis in the previous pages has been upon varying features of payment systems and how these may be differentially preferred in different circumstances. The *amount* of pay which people want from their jobs is the next issue to be examined, and throughout this examination the comparative nature of wants and their satisfaction will be stressed. It is relative position rather than absolute position which determines how we feel about our pay. We form judgements about how much we receive in comparison to others, and we balance this information against judgements of relative skill, effort, age and so on.

Several recent theories are based upon the comparability between different people's relative rewards and relative costs. Homans (1961) developed the notion of 'distributive justice' around a general 'norm of reciprocity': people come to share opinions about how rewards should be distributed among people in relation to the contributions they make. Members of a group who expend time and energy to help the group achieve its goals deserve to be rewarded through status, respect and privileges; people who work harder deserve to earn more than others; people who devote years of their life to a company deserve special treatment. Homans suggested that our shared expectancies about the fair distribution of society's rewards may be thought of in terms of comparisons between ratios of inputs and rewards: a person expects that the ratio of his rewards relative to his inputs (such as responsibility, training or length of service) should be about the same as other people's ratios.

Yet in practice Homans had little to say about the detailed operation of this obviously plausible idea. Patchen (1961) took the details somewhat further, and his examination was specifically concerned with wage comparisons. His model, like that of Homans, focused upon comparisons between ratios. Patchen suggested that a person feels that he is fairly paid when two perceived ratios are consonant. These ratios are 'my pay divided by his pay', where 'he' is a relevant comparison person, and 'my score on dimensions related to pay divided by his score on these dimensions', where 'these dimensions' are defined in terms of skill, effort, working conditions, hours of work and so on. In these terms people want more pay if they are receiving relatively less than is warranted by their scores on features through which their jobs might be evaluated.

Adams (1963, 1965) has put forward similar proposals

under the title of 'equity theory'. This has aroused much interest because it incorporates predictions about behaviour which are similar to those deriving from cognitive dissonance theory. It is assumed that people will take steps to resolve perceived inequity, perhaps by working harder or more carefully if they are relatively overpaid or by lower quantity or quality if they are relatively underpaid.

The many studies generated by these possibilities (see Lawler, 1968, 1971; Pritchard, 1969; and Weick, 1966, for reviews) will not be discussed here for two reasons. Firstly, we are primarily concerned to understand mental processes rather than behaviour so that our interest is mainly upon how judgements of equity or inequity arise rather than upon their consequences. Secondly, the course of development of these studies has taken them out of the field of applied psychology into the realms of pure laboratory research. Studies usually involve undergraduate students hired for the occasion, and inequity is induced by alleging lower competence or by making particularly gross overpayments. Such research has merit for clarifying some relevant issues, but the applicability of its results to organizational situations with their greater complexity and longer time-scale is very dubious.

An example of field research which bears upon equity theory is the study by Hulin (1966). He measured work orientations in 300 offices carrying out the same relatively low-paid jobs, and analysed satisfaction measures in relation to community prosperity. Employees in more prosperous communities (where social comparisons would indicate a personal input–reward discrepancy) were significantly less satisfied with their pay, work and company than those in less wealthy communities.

Amount of pay

There is ample evidence that people receiving higher pay are more satisfied with what they receive (e.g. Opsahl and Dunnette, 1966; Vroom, 1964). This is not surprising, especially since most studies of this question also varied job level and content to a marked extent. Nevertheless studies restricted to fairly homogeneous groups of manual workers or of white-collar staff do reveal the same pattern when payment is through a timework system (e.g. Lawler and Porter, 1963). Employees performing the same job on *piecework* constitute particularly interesting groups in this context. Research we have conducted with such samples into the relationship between attitude to pay and amount earned has revealed every possible pattern. In some cases the high earners are more satisfied, in others the relationship is negative or zero. Presumably the pattern of attitudes depends upon features of the payment system in question and the ability levels of individual employees, and further research needs to look at the details of these.

It is obvious to anyone with experience of wage claims and collective bargaining that if a very similar group of workers earns more than your own group you want a wage increase. This is the same-inputs-but-different-rewards condition which provides the simplest illustration of distributive justice norms. What about comparisons between groups of different inputs? Patchen (1961) showed how equity theory assumptions about the ratio of input and reward ratios were broadly supported. He examined judgements about pay which were made relative to different comparison persons. Particularly relevant here was his finding that the greater the similarity between one's own occupational level and that of a person with higher earnings the less was the reported satisfaction with the comparison. This may be interpreted to mean that the more similar are the inputs of the people with whom you compare yourself, the more important is any inequity which is perceived.

Patchen also looked at differences between the employees in his study. People who believed that they had better prospects outside the firm were, for example, more likely to make upward comparisons with other jobs and pay levels. In another analysis people earning relatively little were seen regularly to make comparisons leading to dissatisfaction, irrespective of pressure from colleagues to be dissatisfied. Social pressures did, however, seem to work differentially for better-paid employees: these people made dissonant comparisons mainly when they were encouraged to do so by others. Patchen was mainly interested in why employees select particular types of people against whom to compare their wages, and this question is manifestly a most important one.

Andrews and Henry (1963) examined managers' opinions about their salary and found that people who compared themselves with their subordinates were relatively more dissatisfied than those who made pay comparisons with more senior colleagues. Lawler's (1965) investigation yielded a similar result, but added the relevant finding that managers regularly overestimate the salary level of their subordinates.

Quantity of inputs

The other main component of equity theory concerns the inputs to work. Pay levels themselves are judged relative to how far people *deserve* high or low pay, and a theory of wants in this area must specify the inputs which give rise to judgements of fairness. In practice it is the work-study engineer, personnel manager and trade union official who have set the pace here. Psychologists have rarely looked beyond general notions of personal qualifications or skill levels, and few of them have acknowledged the complexity and importance of the practitioners' job evaluation schemes. These schemes centre upon the identification and relative weighting of job factors associated with fair pay deals. Typical approaches attempt to measure working conditions, skill, responsibility, problem-solving requirements, knowledge, physical effort, length of learning period and so on, and different inputs are considered relevant in different organizations. Some firms attempt to assess work inputs of this kind entirely through the judgements of managerial staff, whereas others institute committees of managers and the employees concerned. Some other features of job evaluation have been noted on page 51, and useful accounts have been presented by Belcher (1965), McBeath and Rands (1969) and others.

A key question both for equity theorists and job evaluation users centres upon who should be compared against whom in terms of those inputs which are deemed relevant. Within a factory all jobs may have to be compared against each other, but it is apparent that people also make wider comparisons.

The engineers watch the boilermakers and the dentists watch the doctors. It seems likely that comparisons with people whose work inputs are similar to your own may be fairly accurate and very important to you (see page 60). But comparisons which are more wide-ranging are probably less accurate and of lower personal significance. The steelworker's comparison of his pay with that of the Chairman of the British Steel Corporation is possibly a good talking-point in the pub but it is unlikely to be of major immediate importance to him; other matters intrude more urgently upon his lifespace.

We may suggest therefore that the notion of psychological distance is crucial to any comparison theory; people most often and most easily compare themselves to others who are similar to them. In addition it appears that people on similar wages whose perceived inputs to work are *less* than your own may be of greatest concern to you (see page 61); as the differential between others' rewards and your own is perceived to be inequitable so does your desired increase become greater, but this effect is particularly marked for people against whom you compare yourself whose inputs are apparently less than your own.

The number of research investigations in this area is lamentably small, and a greater concentration of effort here is very desirable. So too is an increase in work by psychologists in the field of collective bargaining. The practical difficulties in applying any comparison model of wage levels are both enormous and fascinating. A competent trade union or management bargainer will draw comparisons with many other jobs both inside and outside the factory and in terms of many different work inputs. A major difficulty is for both sides to agree on the facts: the firm down the road might indeed have just paid out a £2 week rise, but what productivity clauses were attached and how has the work changed recently? There will almost always be room for doubt in some of these comparisons, and we need to learn how agreements on what is fair emerge from the varied and misty comparisons between people and inputs that are the essence of collective bargaining. Equity theory contains many basic truths and is straightforward in principle; in practice it becomes complex and difficult.

One line of development which has aroused psychologists' interest is Jaques's theory of equitable payment. Jaques (e.g. 1956, 1961, 1964) distinguishes between two major aspects of work: its discretionary and its prescribed content. Prescribed work is in terms of concrete, specific regulations and procedures; by definition people cannot choose what to do. The discretionary content of a job is, in contrast, dependent upon individual choice and judgement: by using their discretion job-holders necessarily take responsibility for the work. Jaques argues that variations between jobs in this discretionary element should be the major determinant of variations in wage levels.

How then should the discretionary content of jobs be measured? Jaques introduces the interesting notion of 'time-span of discretion'. Basically this is a question of how long you can continue in a role before your superior can be sure that you have been exercising substandard discretion. In some jobs your mistakes show up almost immediately, whereas in others the outcomes of your actions may not be open to evaluation for months or years. Jaques has developed comprehensive definitions and measurement procedures and has applied the time-span of discretion approach in a number of organizations.

The intricacies of his approach will not be examined here, but its broader aspects warrant serious consideration. In effect Jaques is propounding a single-factor job evaluation scheme in terms of time. The pay rewards from jobs should be proportional to their inputs, so that a process of comparison between jobs is necessarily involved; but the inputs are encapsulated in the notion of responsibility, so that other possible factors of comparison are excluded. Jaques does not deny that other aspects of jobs are psychologically relevant when people think about their pay, but he claims that time-span of discretion is the best overall summary of these features.

Bargaining as traditionally conceived is for this reason ruled out; a wages structure which is built up through apparently objective means is not open to dispute in terms outside its own framework. Not surprisingly this idea meets with objections from both unions and managers, and Jaques's schemes for nationwide job evaluation in terms of time-span of discretion have been received with some coolness. So what evidence is there that TSD (the usual abbreviation for time-span of discretion) is the best measure of job worth? Jaques claims that there exists a widespread norm of fairness according to which people consciously or unconsciously recognize how jobs should be valued. He suggests that this norm may be difficult to tap, but introduces attempts to measure people's 'felt-fair pay' – the amount that they feel is fair for a particular job, irrespective of the actual payment which is attached to it. Felt-fair pay (FFP) should on this basis turn out to be strongly related to TSD.

Jaques claims to have found such an association, although many writers have criticized the lack of detail in his presentations of evidence. It is clear that investigators may have difficulty measuring the central concepts, since Jaques himself specifies a four- to six-week training period for those wishing to measure TSD. A study in this field by Richardson (1971) is particularly substantial. He took thirty different measures of input and reward for 180 managerial jobs, and produced an impressive array of intercorrelations and high reliabilities. Of special relevance here was the fact that FFP (measured through an individual's own judgements) correlated +0·86 with TSD (assessed through information provided by his boss). Atchison and French (1967) examined the jobs of 108 scientists and engineers. They found a correlation of +0·90 between these same two measures, and showed that the TSD index was in fact closely associated with job values derived from an orthodox evaluation scheme ($r = +0{\cdot}82$).

It does appear that there is some validity in Jaques's claims, at least as far as white-collar employees are concerned. The TSD measure of responsibility serves as a good measure of an important input to work and it could be used as one component of a job evaluation scheme. Both managers and unionists are however likely to want the incorporation of other components and to wish to maintain their freedom to negotiate about these (c.f. Fox, 1966; Hellriegel and French, 1969). More generally they tend to be deterred by Jaques's writings, since their whole work experience makes it difficult to accept his rejection of their negotiating skills and his insistence that people really have an unconscious cultural norm of fairness.

Changes in aspiration level

The discussion so far has stressed the interpersonal comparisons which are central to pay judgements: people want more or are satisfied relative to the amounts paid to others. We have examined comparisons of inputs (type of work, skill level, etc.) and of rewards (amount of pay), and have illustrated some advances in understanding. Two further factors underlying attitudes to pay should also be mentioned; these will be set in a more general context in Chapter 8 when we review models of motivation.

The first factor is general across the board. It is repeatedly observed that, irrespective of any interpersonal comparisons, people want more pay for their present jobs. This is of course quite understandable in terms of pressing financial commitments and rises in the cost of living, but it may also be interpreted in terms of rising aspiration levels. People have a generalized expectancy that as they become older, at least up to middle age, their material standard of living should improve rather than decline.

Another important determinant of the intensity of wants is their probability of satisfaction. It is a central assumption of theories of achievement motivation (e.g. Atkinson and Feather, 1966; McClelland, 1961; Weiner, 1972) that rewards with a moderate probability of attainment are particularly attractive. Notwithstanding the inevitable comparisons with other people and with general circumstances, people can sometimes perceive that their wants have no chance of being attained. In such conditions it appears that the comparisons can lose their emotional significance, at least for the time being.

This is illustrated through the operation of a 'pay freeze'. In a situation where a freeze is widely accepted within a society, so that virtually all members recognize that their pay cannot be increased, inequitable comparisons with other people are tolerated (c.f. Hinrichs, 1969). Another illustration comes from changes in a firm's profitability: in financially successful times a company's employees will want their inequitable comparisons with other people to be rectified, but in times of zero profit these wishes may be put into abeyance.

In broader perspective, people's attitudes towards pay are central to any industrial-relations culture. Within a factory, region or country employees develop shared interests and concerns about the operation of payment schemes. In recent years government policies have, for example, been particularly salient in the thinking of trade unionists and employers. Adherence to a 'pay norm' or the restoration of free collective bargaining emerge as issues with their own symbolic significance over and above the content of any specific dispute. Wants and feelings about pay regularly spill over into relationships at work which on the face of it have nothing to do with financial considerations.

During 1972 and 1973 in the United Kingdom, for instance, a pattern of go-slows, strikes, grievances and 'working without enthusiasm' was clearly associated with employees' attempts to maintain their standard of living in the face of inflation. These disputes gave rise to polarization and us-and-them feelings which extended well beyond any concern for money. There can be no doubt that feelings about wages influence the quality of life at work in a host of different ways. Further specification of these influences is an important task for the future.

4 Interpersonal relations at work

Research into interpersonal relations, both inside and outside the work environment, is extensive. We have already introduced aspects of this in discussing the Hawthorne studies (see page 27) and in stressing the social comparisons involved in judgements about the adequacy of pay levels (see page 57). Other aspects to be discussed include superior–subordinate relationships (Chapter 5), work-group autonomy (Chapter 6) and role stress (Chapter 7).

We are here concerned to examine more generally how group processes influence well-being at work. Let us start by accepting the obvious, that people want to be with others, and by linking this with the fact that social groupings are inevitable both in work and outside. A work organization is itself a system of social groups with overlapping membership. Each of these groups has a series of objectives, some formally established by the organization and some informally self-generated. These objectives serve to guide the activities of each group, but they also illustrate the kinds of satisfaction which people want from their social life at work. The first part of this chapter is a review of some of the social functions of the work-group.

The social functions of the work-group

Contact with others

There can be little doubt that people's thoughts and actions are directed primarily to other people. One study (Cameron *et al.*, 1973) analysed the topics in the thoughts of over 4,000 Americans, and found that in the vast majority of cases it was other people who formed the object of thought. Factor-analytic studies of job satisfaction repeatedly demonstrate the presence of strong 'other people' factors (see Cross, 1973; Herzberg *et al.*, 1957; Vroom, 1964; Warr and Routledge, 1969). In a similar vein we might imagine that employees discussing with their husband or wife the recent happenings at work will devote most attention to what other colleagues have done and less time to the performance of the equipment with which they work. Following this example through, we might envisage that discussions will cover unpleasant behaviour by colleagues as well as the good things that have happened and been said.

We should therefore go beyond the assertion that social interaction is attractive because it brings us in contact with other people whom we like. This is no doubt part of its value to us, but in broader perspective it is essential as a stimulus to mental activity or behaviour. Most of the theories of motivation touched on in this book support the notion that people have a fundamental need to seek out variety and stimulation from their environment; this need is clearly reflected in social interaction.

It is nevertheless apparent that liking is more pleasant than disliking and work-group membership carries with it the possibility that friendships may develop. Studies of interpersonal judgement have drawn attention to the fact that people tend to like others more than they dislike them (e.g. Boucher and Osgood, 1969; Warr, 1971b). Other research (see Lott and Lott, 1965, for a summary) has examined the factors which lead to liking, and some of these deserve mention here.

Physical proximity and the social interaction which typically follows have regularly been found to create some degree of interpersonal attraction. The reverse can of course happen – neighbours at home and at work do come to dislike each other – but it appears that in very general terms people in contact with each other will enjoy their company more than they will dislike each other. In part such an effect arises from the emergence of perceived similarities of interests, attitudes and behaviour, since such perceived similarity is a strong source of interpersonal attraction; conversely people who like each other tend to *assume* more similarity than often exists.

A related source of attraction comes from a recognition that other people accept and value you. In one sense this is hardly surprising, since people who express their appreciation of you are naturally preferable to those who insult and denigrate you. The point is worth making in order to link this discussion with the arguments of existential theorists such as Binswanger (1963) and May (1967). These authors emphasize the ultimate aloneness of each individual. They believe that one of man's most basic needs is to bridge the distance between himself and other people by some form of relationship which breaks the boundaries constraining him as a person (e.g. Hampden-Turner, 1971).

It may seem a big jump from existentialist ideas about the loneliness of the individual to the humdrum world of work. The suggestion that work provides a means of bridging the interpersonal gap is not one open to controlled empirical validation; it rests more upon evidence from individual reflection. The possible meaning of a work-group to its members is captured well in this account by an apprentice:

> As soon as [the chargehand] had gone the workers near me extended the unforgettable claustrophobic comradeship of the factory. It is a friendship generated of common experience, common income and common worktasks. Out of this shared pattern of experience grows a common culture of the workplace. And like other cultures it can never be fully understood by the outsider . . . On that first morning at work I began to learn all the expected patterns of response, all the rewards and sanctions, just as an infant learns its native tongue. I quickly learned the harsh language of aggressive friendship; the need to identify myself with the workgroup in opposition to all forms of authority from the chargehand up. Nothing must be allowed to threaten the cohesion of the workers, for only through this 'sticking together' could we solve the problems facing us [Fraser, 1969, p. 24].

Social comparison

A second work-group function may be illustrated through Festinger's (1954) theory of social comparison processes. This asserts that people want to compare their opinions and abilities with others. In some cases they can obtain fairly objective information about their position (for instance, by athletic competion), but in very many areas they have to rely on more uncertain knowledge arising from social encounters. These encounters provide opportunities for comparisons between oneself and others, and in part they are steered by participants with this in mind. People are often unsure about the validity of their own beliefs about social and personal issues and they take comfort from learning about their comparability with other people's beliefs.

These ideas are extremely powerful in an explanatory sense, since a great deal of behaviour in society can be interpreted through them (e.g. Festinger, 1957; Kelvin, 1970). The use of other people's judgements for testing one's own view of reality is particularly well illustrated by experiments into the autokinetic effect. A pin-prick of light in an otherwise completely dark environment appears to be in motion even when it is in fact stationary, a phenomenon known as autokinesis. Sherif (1935) capitalized on this extremely ambiguous situation to explore the effect of group factors on individual judgements. He asked people to estimate how far the light had moved during a specific period of time. This they did alone and subsequently as a member of a group. It was found that individuals who initially diverged in their judgements moved towards agreement, or a 'norm of judgement', in the group situation. Indeed most individuals faced with unanimity of judgement among their fellow group members about an ambiguous situation will accept the group norms as correct (Sherif and Sherif, 1956; Asch, 1951). In general, the more ambiguous the circumstances, the greater will be the conformity of behaviour (e.g. Shaw, 1971). These laboratory worlds may seem the ultimate in simplicity, but people's reliance upon others for understanding reality has been regularly noted in much more complex environments. We seek out social relationships which can diminish our personal doubts and support our prejudices, and we adjust our beliefs and perceptions in order to reduce marked conflicts with people we value. Several features of these processes recur throughout this chapter, and their significance in the work situation should perhaps be highlighted at this point.

Anyone who is in contact with others at work learns something from them which bears upon his concept of himself and upon what it is appropriate for him to think or do. Social comparisons may be of a general non-work kind, but they regularly concern a person's views about features of his job. Unsure about how he feels towards the foreman, the union, the canteen, the allowance for weekend work or how to react to being transferred to another machine, he can gain clarity and possibly a coherent view from his workmates. The essence of social comparison theory and others like it is that people *want* in their thinking to set their views in the context of those held by others and that they *want* to use others to reduce their own uncertainty. In part, then, social contact at work helps people to decide what is personally real or true.

One other aspect of social comparison should be mentioned here. In addition to comparing their opinions and abilities with those of others, people continually compare their own wants and the satisfaction of these with their perceptions of other people's wants and levels of satisfaction. We are often unsure what we should want and whether we are satisfied, and our estimates of other people's satisfaction can be crucial reference points as we seek to reduce uncertainty.

The development of norms

Our social construction of reality may further be seen in the development within groups of norms or shared values. All special groups acquire views of their own about what members should do, think and feel. Work-group norms may cover standards of quality or quantity (e.g. Mechanic, 1962; Whyte 1955; Zaleznik, Christensen and Roethlisberger, 1958), time-keeping or holiday scheduling. They often extend to methods of structuring encounters (Can I just walk in? Do I call him 'Mr'?) and to the views people hold about the products made by their company.

Social psychologists have a lot to say about norms and their role in society (e.g. Berg and Bass, 1961; Hollander, 1967; Homans, 1961; Kelvin, 1970; Krech, Crutchfield and Ballachey,

1962). Three points will, however, suffice for this brief treatment. First, the fact that people actively want some norms is a central theme of this section. Our perceived world must be structured and organized, at least up to a point. Colleagues at work help in this respect just as do other people. Second, we should note the close interconnection between the concepts of 'norm' and 'cohesiveness'. A cohesive group is one whose members value each other and their membership in the group. It is well established that cohesive groups tend to adhere most strongly to their norms (see the discussion of quota restriction on page 50), and the direction of causality between cohesiveness and norm establishment is presumably two-way. This is a feature which will be taken up in the next section.

The third aspect of the operation of norms in a group is their association with status. Some degree of conformity is usually required if a person is to gain some informal status in a group. With this status goes potential influence and the group's permission to deviate more than may lower-status people. Members of a group often tacitly recognize this and may value status for the 'idiosyncracy credit' which it brings (Hollander, 1958) – the group's permission to be different from the majority. This is not to say that people are continually striving and competing with each other, for informally accepted 'pecking-orders' are regularly established in which lower-status people are quite happy with their lot. The point which is important here is that people also want status for quite different reasons – those related to the earlier discussion about social comparison. Recognition of your status within the groups to which you belong helps to clarify your assessment of yourself and to set up expected ways of responding to new situations: status hierarchies may be desirable for the way they give a structure to our mental and behavioural repertoires.

In practice of course there are several hierarchies within most groups. Major individual or social factors such as age, job, social presence, sex or nationality can be reflected in separate rankings, and it is usual for some consistency to develop between these rankings: people of high standing on one factor may be of high standing on others. Such a balanced situation is one of 'status congruence', and several studies have suggested that people want congruence rather than incongruence in their status relationships (see Golembiewski, 1965; Korman, 1971b). Incongruent relationships tend to generate stress reactions which may be viewed in terms similar to those suggested by Kahn *et al.* (1964) in their interpretations of role conflict (see Chapter 7).

Goal-achievement

The dimensions of the work-group which have been examined so far have primarily concerned an individual's establishment of some socially validated understanding of himself and the people around him. A different set of satisfactions derives from the achievement of formal and informal goals. Effective operation and goal-achievement is in itself valued by most people at work (e.g. Herzberg *et al.*, 1957), and there are many processes where this kind of success is only possible through group membership and interdependence. A section of a work organization may be charged with producing so many radios, with cutting so much coal or with administering certain social security benefits. These and other tasks cannot be completed by an individual on his own, and group membership takes on value as a means to an end in goal-achievement. Take for instance the following account provided by a chargehand responsible for a group of men on a rolling mill: 'The highlight of my time last year was when me and my group got together and decided to break the record for the amount of steel rolled by one shift. We worked ourselves to a standstill just to get more out than anyone had before. It wasn't the money we would get for extra work, it was more the feeling that you, as a group, were better than others.' Our social wants at work may thus also have their roots in our motivation to achieve some results from our activities to which we attach personal value and significance (e.g. McClelland *et al.*, 1953; McClelland, 1961; McClelland and Winter, 1969).

The goals which we try to attain at work are of course not only formally prescribed ones. Workers can better assert their wishes in the face of management demands if they take advantage of the power deriving from group solidarity. Different styles of bargaining behaviour in 'strategic' versus 'erratic' groups have for instance been illustrated by Sayles (1958). Women employees are often believed to appreciate the opportunity for talking which work-group membership provides, and male employees may jointly enter competitions or place racing bets. We may get new information from our work colleagues about the performance and price of cars, about changes to be made in the city centre and about whatever catches our collective interest.

Conclusion

This section has attempted to identify some of the wants which are satisfied through social contact at work. Interpersonal relationships are seen to matter for fundamental reasons of self-evaluation and to meet our intrinsic needs for variety, stimulation and achievement. Interpersonal needs are not simply a question of wishing to be with people you like, although the chance of friendship is a strong motive in many people. Such friendships can arise from a work situation but commonly extend beyond it.

Research workers have a long way to go in mapping out individual and situational variations in wants of the kind noted here. One group of employees which has been thought to lay particular stress on the social attractions of work is that of part-time women employees. It is notable that more than a third of women workers are employed on a part-time basis (Department of Employment, 1973), and comparisons between the patterns of their work-motives and those of full-time women employees would repay further study. More generally, work is becoming increasingly feminized: the working population of Britain has increased by 1·3 million in the past twenty years, and all of these are women. The population of male workers has in fact declined by 45,000 in this period, and women now constitute around 36 per cent of the working population. Cherns (1975), in discussing these trends, points out that a central feature of working-class culture has long been the acquisition of masculinity through work and work-groups.

Changes in this, as work becomes less physically demanding and women achieve more positions of responsibility, will be worth investigation.

An important distinction running through much of the preceding discussion is between the formal and informal systems of work-organization. The formal system has as its elements work-activities and relationships which pertain to the organization's major functions (making ships, selling furniture, publishing newspapers, etc.). The informal system grows up around the personal relationships and non-work activities which are present within any work setting. Some of the interpersonal wants described in the previous pages are satisfied through the formal system, others through the informal system or through the overlapping operation of the two.

This distinction may be rephrased in terms of 'task groups' and 'sentient groups' (Miller and Rice, 1967). Task groups are those which are formally established for a specific organizational purpose, whereas sentient or feeling groups are those which develop informally out of social interaction at work. It is easily seen that marked conflict between task and sentient groups can present operational difficulties.

Yet there are usually built-in conflicts between the technical and social requirements of a job. Chapter 2 illustrated how the technical enthusiasm of scientific management had to be tempered by a recognition of employees' social needs. A concept which embraces both aspects of organization is that of a 'socio-technical system' (e.g. Rice, 1958; Trist *et al.*, 1963). The idea here is that any working organization is a combination of technological elements (the formal task, the physical conditions, layout of work, equipment available, and so on) and social networks among those who perform the work. The technology and the social system are in mutual interaction with each other, and to some extent each determines the other. In understanding an organization, or in managing it, we have to think not only in technical, material and financial terms but also in terms of the wants, values, expectations and norms of the people within it. Just as an organization cannot aim entirely to maximize member satisfaction, so must it avoid attempting only to maximize technical efficiency. Similarly the worth or effectiveness of an organization should be seen neither in technical nor in social terms alone, but in terms of its socio-technical entirety. This theme is further developed on pages 165 to 167.

Some characteristics of work-groups

After this general introduction to the bases of interpersonal relations in work, we turn now to examine some studies of work-group characteristics. The characteristics in question are cohesiveness, similarity of members, size, social support and bureaucratic emphasis.

Cohesiveness

The relationship between the cohesiveness of groups and their adherence to norms was introduced in general terms in the previous section. Here we shall look at research specifically directed to the cohesiveness of groups in working organizations. One strand of this research has concentrated upon norms of quota restriction in payment-by-results groups (see Chapter 3, page 50), illustrating how more cohesive groups establish and stick closely to production quotas (e.g. Seashore, 1954; Whyte, 1955) and how rate-busters (employees exceeding their quota) often differ from other group members through their cultural backgrounds or personality and value systems (e.g. Zaleznik, Christensen and Roethlisberger, 1958). The fact that cohesiveness may be associated with norms of working harder as well as of restriction was classically demonstrated by Berkowitz (1954) and Schachter *et al.* (1951).

We need to inquire more deeply into the question of why people want to be in cohesive work-groups. That they often do want this was shown in a study by Van Zelst (1952). He gave seventy-four carpenters and bricklayers on a building site the chance to make three choices of work-partner and work-groups were reconstituted on the basis of these choices. Not surprisingly the complexity of this operation left some employees without their first or second choice, but the majority were so partnered. Productivity was found to rise during the subsequent months, and overall job satisfaction also increased significantly. Similar results have been reported by Goodacre (1951, 1953).

Increased satisfaction here was no doubt partly due to increased enjoyment of friendly company. As in all studies in this area, however, the mere fact that management saw fit to take notice of employees' preferences is also likely to have contributed to positive reactions. A third possible factor arises from the interdependence which was a necessary feature of each work-group (cf. Lodahl and Porter, 1961). People may 'work together' in the sense that they are in close proximity without contributing to each other's success or failure at the job. In such relatively independent work situations, people may well prefer likeable to dislikeable colleagues for all the obvious and less obvious reasons noted above. But in groups with a built-in task interdependence people may also choose others because they are skilful or able to complement the abilities they themselves possess. Such a basis for choosing is likely to account partly for the typically observed preference for being allowed to choose work-partners.

This may be illustrated through a study by Cross and Warr (1971) in the packing department of a factory making chocolate and sugar confectionery. The work-force of this department comprised thirty-five operatives, three supervisors and a manager. All of these were women. The operatives packed chocolates into boxes which moved on one of two conveyor belts, and payment was on a group bonus scheme for each belt. The speed at which a belt moved was in principle determined by a team's supervisor, but her decision was naturally constrained by the ability of the slower members in the team.

As is common with women workers, the age distribution of the group of packers was bimodal: nineteen were under 24 years old and sixteen were over 35. Employees' intelligence test scores were negatively associated with age (the older people scoring less) and were closely related to independently obtained supervisory assessments of job skill. In the first stage of the investigation each employee's feelings about her work were assessed through structured interviews which yielded scores on six separate attitude dimensions – those concerning working conditions, the job itself, pay, supervision, relations with co-workers and the firm as a whole. Sociometric data of the kind recorded by Van Zelst were also obtained.

It emerged from analyses of this material that the employees who were most unhappy about their job were the younger, more intelligent, more skilled individuals. It is of interest here that their dissatisfaction was focused upon their pay levels and upon the packing job itself; in other respects their attitudes were as positive as those of the older workers. In practice what the younger group wanted was the opportunity to work faster and to earn higher wages. This was achieved by reconstituting the work-groups in terms of skill, and allowing each belt to work at its preferred speed.

Such an adjustment resulted in more favourable attitudes in both groups. The younger, more skilled employees immediately began to earn more through the group bonus scheme, and their satisfaction with pay naturally increased. The older group initially worked rather more slowly, but in response to adjustments in style of supervision which were now possible they too gradually increased their output and satisfaction. The significant point here is that both groups came to express much more positive feelings about their colleagues.

Group cohesiveness is thus wanted for social contact reasons of the kind noted earlier in this chapter (the content of the younger women's conversation at work was, not surprisingly, quite different from that of the older women), but it may also be desired for non-social reasons to do for example with better task-achievement and higher pay.

In some work situations people's preferences for colleagues are routinely allowed to influence the composition of work groups. Sales staff or clerical workers are often allowed some choice of work-partner. Chadwick-Jones (1969) has described how traditional Welsh steelworks operated a self-selection procedure through the employees' trade union. In steelworks with which we are familiar, the promotion ladder in, for example, the melting-shop is a clearly established one so that members can only advance within their present team. Members of a team determine who shall join it, and management and senior operatives review annually how well the members of each team are operating together. It is such a concern for interpersonal relationships which is often thought to distinguish traditional industries from the more modern, impersonal ones.

Similarity of members

A closely related strand of research which deserves mention here is that to do with the homogeneity of group membership. The illustrations in the previous section have argued that people want some similarity in social and non-social characteristics, but the examples have mainly been drawn from groups of manual workers. A separate series of studies has looked at interpersonal relationships in non-manual, problem-solving groups. Schutz (1955) was particularly concerned with a dimension of member 'personalness–counterpersonalness'. This refers to people's liking or not liking warm interpersonal relations and mutual dependency. By establishing groups in terms of their compatibility on this dimension he was able to examine its influence on social behaviour and satisfaction. Schutz's main findings were in terms of the increased problem-solving effectiveness of compatible groups (made up either of personal or of counterpersonal members), but he also obtained evidence that such groups were rated more favourably by members than were incompatible teams.

Other studies of compatibility in problem-solving groups have also been directed primarily at how effectively they perform their work or at the way people interact with each other, rather than at the preference of members (see Cooper and Mangham, 1971; Collins and Raven, 1969; Haythorn, 1968; Heslin, 1964; and Stogdill, 1959, for reviews). This means that the links between member similarity and interpersonal satisfaction have been established only in outline. A possible interpretation of the literature is that similarity or cohesiveness are mainly important when they are absent: once they are present at some minimal level, increases in one form of similarity (personalness, for instance) are traded off in members' evaluations for other forms of complementarity (task knowledge, for example). Beyond a minimal level increasingly high similarity within work-groups has in general no further influence on interpersonal evaluations.

Group size

A feature of groups which is more easily measured is their size, and several investigations have examined the influence of this upon member attitudes. The summary by Porter and Lawler (1965) leaves little doubt that people prefer to belong to small work-units (see also Indik, 1965; and Wicker, McGrath and Armstrong, 1972). They become more active within small groups and are more likely to develop a sense of personal commitment to the group. It is, however, important to distinguish between the size of a work-unit and that of an overall organization: for immediate work-units the pattern of wants in relation to size is clear, but size of an organization as a whole is less obviously reflected in employees' attitudes (e.g. Hall, 1972).

Social support

Several of the work-group characteristics already noted bear upon the degree to which social support is provided between group members. Differences in membership and structure can be reflected in a varying potential for comfort and assistance in difficult times. Many work situations are stressful in ways which will be examined in Chapter 7, and people's ability to cope with stress is clearly mediated by the support which is available from their colleagues.

This theme was classically illustrated in a study of work-group organization among coal-miners (Trist and Bamforth, 1951; Trist *et al.*, 1963). Two types of work organization were studied, built around the 'shortwall' and 'longwall' approaches to the job. The shortwall system, the traditional organization in British coal-mines, was based upon small teams ranging in size from two to eight men. The teams were assembled on the basis of mutual compatibility. In their work they were highly autonomous, each team being responsible for the mining of a small section of the coal-face. This included the cutting, loading and removal of the coal. Within each team individuals helped one another according to the requirements of the situation and, partly because of the dangers and anxieties of working underground in the dark, lasting friendships among team members developed.

For engineering and technical reasons it became desirable to change the organization of work in the mines. With more sophisticated equipment a different work-group was required, operating according to what was termed the longwall system. New groups comprising between forty and fifty men under a single supervisor were formed. Each large group was then divided into three shifts, each of which was responsible for different aspects of the coal-mining process. The three shifts working on the same coal-face would not meet at work, hence communication between them was severely restricted. Yet they were functionally highly interdependent since the efficiency with which one shift could carry out its work depended upon the prior shift having completed its tasks satisfactorily. Additionally, the work in the longwall system was spread across coal-faces typically 180 to 200 yards across. The physical distance between team members combined with the prevailing darkness functioned to reduce social interaction. Not surprisingly, with such a wide physical spread between team members, problems of supervision arose.

The miners who experienced the longwall system did not like it: feelings of meaninglessness, social isolation and passivity increased, and a norm of low productivity was adopted. Indeed the effects were so marked that further changes to the work organization were soon introduced. The men were regrouped so that all the aspects of the mining process were carried out by each shift. As a result better relations between those doing the different tasks arose and there was more variety of work. The situation began to improve.

Clearly, the longwall system as initially implemented had disrupted the social organization of the miners to such an extent that this potentially superior mining process could not work efficiently. The new organization was physically arranged such that it was difficult for the men to set up an informal organization which met their emotional needs. These findings were interpreted by Trist and his colleagues in terms of variations in socio-technical systems (see page 75). The changes created by the longwall method did not only affect cohesiveness, however. As Emery and Trist (1960, p. 91) observe:

> Nor does it appear that the basic psychological needs being met by the grouping are workers' needs for friendship on the job, as is frequently postulated by advocates of better 'human relations' in industry. Grouping produces its main psychological effects when it leads to a system of work roles such that the workers are primarily related to each other by way of the requirements of task performance and task interdependence. When this task orientation is established the worker should find that he has an adequate range of mutually supportive roles (mutually supportive with respect to performance and to carrying stress that arises from the task).

It is clear that the need for social support varies from job to job: coal-mining is particularly stressful. Clearly also, people differ in their requirements for social support; Powell (1973) has shown how older miners are particularly likely to be found on coal-faces with group working.

Bureaucratic emphasis

Most writers on groups and organizations have drawn attention to a major dimension of difference which we might refer to here as degree of bureaucratic emphasis. Weber's (1947) discussion of bureaucracy stressed the existence of impersonal rules, the division of labour, a hierarchical structure, a concern for tradition and similar characteristics. Burns and Stalker (1961) identified 'mechanistic' and 'organismic' structures. Their extreme types may be characterized in this way:

Mechanistic	*Organismic*
1 Great division of labour and specialist tasks	1 The person with the specialist knowledge goes where he is needed

2 Clear hierarchy of authority	2 Authority is vested in the person who can deal with the problem whoever he is
3 Precise definition of job, duties, rules, etc.	3 Continual re-definition of individuals' jobs as the situation requires
4 Centralization of information and decision-making	4 Information and knowledge may be located anywhere in the organizational network
5 Preponderance of vertical communication	5 Preponderance of horizontal communication

A more detailed formulation based on factor analytic treatment of empirically obtained organizational data by Pugh, Hickson and Hinings (1969) suggested that full bureaucratization may be defined in terms of high scores on three major dimensions. These are:

(i) structuring of activities – the degree to which the behaviour of employees is specified by dividing work into specialist jobs, laying down standardized routines and procedures and by formalizing written records, etc.;

(ii) concentration of authority – the degree to which authority to take decisions is concentrated at the top of the organization;

(iii) line control of work-flow – the degree to which control is exercised through impersonal procedures rather than at the discretion of employees.

There are important points of detail distinguishing these and other writers (see Hall, 1972; and Payne and Pugh, 1971, 1975, for summaries), but they generally agree that organizations and work-groups can differ in the emphasis they place on bureaucratic values. The question of importance here is: how far do employees want an emphasis of this kind?

Quite obviously some structuring of activities is necessary in any group, but a very wide range of variation is possible. Although there have been many discussions concerning the degree to which bureaucratic emphasis is or is not appropriate in terms of efficiency, there appear to have been few inquiries into employees' preferences. One fact is, however, clear. Just as organizations differ in this characteristic, so do individuals have widely varying degrees of bureaucratic orientation. The attitude–personality syndrome of authoritarianism, identified by Adorno *et al.* (1950), is clearly a central one which affects the value we attach to institutional structuring. More recently Gordon (1970) has developed a measure of an individual's 'bureaucratic orientation'. This concept is intended to be the personal analogue of the organizational characteristic, and taps areas like these:

Self-subordination: a willingness to comply fully with the stated wishes of a superior and to have decisions made for one by higher authority.

Compartmentalization: a preference for impersonal or formal relationships with others on the job, particularly with individuals at different organizational levels.

Rule conformity: a desire for the security that the following of rules, regulations, and standard operating procedures affords.

Traditionalism: a need for the security provided by organizational identification and conformity to the in-group norm.

Individual bureaucratic orientation is highly correlated with the broader syndrome of authoritarianism, and has been found to be associated with a preference for institutional bureaucracy in several studies. For instance, Gordon reports that high scorers are more likely to remain working for bureaucratic organizations. Our own studies with nurses and local-authority employees have suggested that more bureaucratically oriented people are likely to be more satisfied with their work situation generally.

The characteristics of formal organizations and employees' reactions to them have been extensively discussed by Argyris (e.g. 1957, 1962, 1973). He points out how the traditional bureaucratic emphasis tends to inhibit personal risk-taking and experimentation, the pursuit of new ideas and information, a trust in and concern for other members, and how it tends to encourage people to deny personal responsibility for their actions. Argyris is clear that different personalities should be comfortable in different environments, and that there is no single 'best' kind of organization.

Nevertheless there are *a priori* reasons for viewing self-expression, creativity, trust in others and willingness to accept personal responsibility as desirable. Argyris sees these as leading to 'authentic' relationships between individuals, through allowing the individual to become aware of his needs and abilities and those of other people. In the long term this should lead to greater well-being, and as Korman (1971b) and Shepard (1965) point out work relationships can be of considerable importance in this respect. We must ask whether organizations are in general appropriately structured for such an objective, or whether the level of bureaucratization which occurs serves to hinder the well-being of employees beyond a reasonable level. To reach a generalization about this, more studies of single organizations are required, in which psychological profit and loss are set against effectiveness in financial and technical terms.

5 Participation in decision-making

Mulder (1971) has suggested that 'participation is the most vital organizational problem of our time . . . [It] will change the leadership function of the more powerful; and new structures for leadership, decision-making, and communication will develop . . . For the individual members, feelings of well-being and their sense of self-realization are related to participation and its consequences' (p. 312). This is not a new theme. As early as 1919 the Federation of British Industries recommended that 'workers in every industry should be given the fullest possible voice in the conditions under which they are employed'. Similar recommendations were made in the psychological literature. Myers (1920), for instance, wrote that 'the impartial observer [cannot] deny the justice of workers' demand for greater industrial control in these days of government by consent, of increasing democratic spirit in education, and growth of personality and responsibility' (pp. 176–7); and Brierly (1920), noting a 'demand for control', proposed that 'it is our business to inquire what conditions lie behind the demand, what are the psychological influences which have led to its formation' (p. 224). Whether individuals want to, should or can become involved in decisions made at higher levels within their employing organizations has become an area of inquiry central to those concerned with employee well-being.

'Participation' has taken on several meanings and herein lies a major difficulty in structuring the evidence, since whilst the same word is used by different authors they are often referring to very different processes. Nevertheless it is possible to discern an important distinction between *immediate* and *distant participation* (Strauss and Rosenstein, 1970).

Immediate participation refers to employees' involvement

in matters concerning their everyday work, typically through informal interaction with their immediate superiors. The focus is on employees' influence in supervisory and first-level management decision-making. Research activity around this concept of participation has been extensive. It may be seen as originating with the Hawthorne studies (see Chapter 2, pages 27 to 32) and gaining impetus from the efforts of writers such as Argyris (1957, 1962, 1964), Bennis (1966), Likert (1961, 1967) and McGregor (1960, 1967). (See Strauss, 1968, and Strauss and Rosenstein, 1970, for an elaboration of this argument.) Among the concepts relevant to this approach to participation are 'democratic supervision', 'consideration', 'employee-orientation' and 'participative leadership'. All refer to the extent to which leaders discourage or encourage their immediate subordinates to become involved in, or take responsibility for, decisions relevant to their own work activities. With the emphasis jointly upon employee involvement and superior–subordinate interaction the study of immediate participation overlaps considerably with the study of leadership. We shall consequently use the terms 'immediate participation' and 'participative leadership' interchangeably.

Distant participation, by contrast, refers to employees' involvement in higher levels of organizational decision-making. For practical reasons involvement of this kind is usually achieved through varying forms of representation: employee directors and works councils are examples. The emphasis is upon the involvement of individuals in decisions less directly relevant to their own work but of greater concern to the employing organization as a whole.

In this chapter we shall consider studies concerned with employees' attitudes towards both these kinds of participation.

An illustrative study

A relatively straightforward investigation by Sadler (1966, 1970) serves to illustrate research into immediate participation. This involved 1,270 men and 319 women employed by two companies engaged in the marketing of office and computer equipment and in research and development for computer facilities. Each individual studied the following accounts of possible leadership styles. They represent, from first to last, an increasing degree of subordinate participation.

A. The manager makes his decision promptly and communicates it to his subordinates clearly and firmly. He expects them to carry it out loyally and without raising difficulties.

B. The manager makes his decision promptly, but then tries to get his subordinates' agreement to it before going ahead. He believes in carrying his staff with him rather than issuing orders.

C. The manager does not reach his decisions until he has consulted his subordinates. He listens to their advice, weighs it and then announces his decision. He then expects all to work loyally to implement it irrespective of whether or not it is in accordance with the advice they gave.

D. The manager calls a meeting of his staff whenever there is an important decision to take. He lays the problem before the group and invites discussion. He accepts the majority viewpoint as the decision.

Respondents were then invited to state, on an anonymous questionnaire, (a) which of the styles they would most want to work under, and (b) which style, if any, characterized their own superior. They were also asked to indicate on short scales their overall job satisfaction, satisfaction with their company, and the confidence they had in management.

For ease of reference, Sadler identifies the styles A, B, C and D as 'tells', 'sells', 'consults' and 'joins' respectively. The distribution of preferences and perceptions of one's own superior which he recorded are summarized in Table 5.1.

Amongst men, the 'consults' style is stongly preferred, with 'sells' next. Few male respondents felt they would enjoy working under 'tells' or 'joins' leadership styles. The pattern amongst women is similar, except that the preference for the 'consults' style is less marked. These preferences are however not paralleled in the employees' perceptions of their own managers' actual behaviour. Only 26 and 14 per cent of the men and women respectively saw their managers as using this style. Among the men similar proportions reported that their managers adopted a 'sells' (24 per cent) or a 'tells' (18 per cent) style, or 'none of these' (24 per cent). Only a small minority described their superior as 'joining'. The women described their managers most frequently as 'tells', whilst 24 per cent felt that none of the descriptions applied. Analyses according to job types revealed that the 'consults' style was perceived more often by the more highly qualified employees, whereas the 'tells' and 'sells' styles were endorsed more frequently by their less-well-qualified counterparts. Thus, whilst there was a strong preference for the 'consults' leadership style, this was not encountered in practice as frequently as it was desired.

Table 5.1. The percentage of male and female employees who: (a) prefer each style of leadership; and (b) who perceive their own managers as using each style.

		A: Tells	*B: Sells*	*C: Consults*	*D: Joins*	*None of these*	*No reply*
(a) Preferred Leadership Style	Men	8%	23%	61%	5%	—	2%
	Women	15%	25%	35%	17%	—	8%
(b) Perceived Leadership Style	Men	18%	24%	26%	5%	24%	3%
	Women	29%	14%	14%	6%	24%	13%

Since these employees want 'consultative' bosses, it seems reasonable to assume that they will be generally more satisfied if this is the style of leadership they perceive themselves to be experiencing. Let us look, therefore, at how the different perceived leadership styles relate to overall job satisfaction, satisfaction with the company, and confidence in immediate management. The levels of satisfaction and confidence in management expressed by respondents in relation to the perceived style of their own managers are shown in Table 5.2. The figures reported there represent the average score of the group in question as a percentage of the maximum score possible.

Table 5.2. Job satisfaction, satisfaction with the company and confidence in management in relation to leadership style.

Perceived leadership style	*Overall job satisfaction score*	*Satisfaction with company*	*Confidence in management*
A: Tells	75	82	64
B: Sells	79	85	72
C: Consults	82	87	75
D: Joins	80	85	61
None of these	72	80	49

Across all three measures a reported 'consults' style is associated with higher scores on the other measures. Individuals who see their own managers as 'consultative' are more satisfied with their jobs and their company, and express greater confidence in management. Respondents who feel that none of these styles is an adequate description of their own superior's behaviour express the least favourable attitudes. This last point has been interpreted by Sadler as indicating that the managers so described tend to be inconsistent in their behaviour and that their unpredictability is the source of dissatisfaction.

The findings presented so far illustrate that employees prefer and are more satisfied with the 'consults' style of leadership. The magnitude of this relationship may be augmented, however, by an examination of the congruence between preference and reported style of superior. In other words, are people whose preference and perception coincide more satisfied than the others? The relationship of overall job satisfaction to congruence between perceived and preferred style is presented in Table 5.3.

Clearly employees under the style of leadership they prefer, be it 'telling', 'selling', 'consulting' or 'joining', are more satisfied than those who perceive their manager's behaviour as incongruent with their own preferences.

A number of conclusions are suggested by this study. First, the leadership styles described are meaningful: the vast majority of employees felt able to express a preference, and 71 per cent of all respondents, given the option of stating that

Table 5.3. Perceived and preferred leadership style in relation to job satisfaction.

	Perceived style	*Preferred style*	*Overall job satisfaction score*
CONGRUENCE	Tells	Tells	80
	Sells	Sells	83
	Consults	Consults	83
	Joins	Joins	81
INCONGRUENCE	Tells	Other than Tells	73
	Sells	Other than Sells	78
	Consults	Other than Consults	78
	Joins	Other than Joins	77

none of the four styles applied, still felt that their own manager could be characterized by one of them. Second, the 'consults' style of leadership is the most preferred. Third, the 'consults' style is associated with the more positive attitudes to work. This result is, however, qualified by the finding that 'consults' is the style most wanted by employees. Indeed, the final conclusion is that congruency between perceived and preferred leadership style is associated with higher job satisfaction, regardless of the style in question; and some people do want a 'tells'- or 'sells'-style leader.

This is but a single study, which involves merely one section of the work population. Only by examining participative leadership across many work settings may we gain some knowledge of the generality of these findings. Let us turn to a selection of other investigations into immediate participation.

Correlational research into immediate participation

The most common approach to the study of participative leadership has been based upon a correlational research design. Sadler's study described above exemplifies this method. Typically, investigators have looked for differences in leadership styles across different work situations and have examined the relationship at one point in time between a manager's style and the attitudes of his subordinates.

Baumgartel (1956), using the categories introduced by Lewin, Lippitt and White (1939), identified three styles of leadership amongst laboratory directors. *Laissez-faire* directors were characterized by little contact and minimal mutual influence between themselves and their subordinates. *Directive* leaders were in closer contact with their subordinates, exerted considerable influence over their work activities, but were not influenced by their opinions. Finally, *participative* directors had frequent contact with their subordinates, and were strongly influenced by them. When the work attitudes of the research scientists were examined, it was found that those responsible to *participative* directors expressed more favourable attitudes towards their superiors and their work than did their colleagues whose superiors were *laissez-faire* or *directive*. A similar finding is reported by Weschler, Kahane and Tannenbaum (1952) in a study of employees in a naval research laboratory, and Miller (1967) among industrial scientists and engineers.

A series of investigations conducted at the Survey Research Center in the University of Michigan involved very different groups of employees. Two styles of supervision were identified. *Employee-oriented* supervisors were said to 'allow their employees to work out the details of when and how work will be handled. They do not seem to feel the need to get into the production process at every point to check on how things are going, to make changes, to reassign work, and in other ways to keep a close check on operations' (Katz, Maccoby and Morse, 1950, p. 35). *Production-oriented* supervisors, in contrast, 'check up on their employees more frequently' and 'in general limit their freedom to do the work in their own way' (Kahn and Katz, 1953, p. 617). The relationship of employee attitudes to these two supervisory styles was investigated in several organizations, for instance in an insurance company (Katz, Maccoby and Morse, 1950), railway maintenance sections (Katz, Maccoby, Gurin and Floor, 1951) and a car factory (Katz, 1963; Jacobson, 1951). The findings were generally consistent: those working under employee-oriented supervisors expressed greater satisfaction with their work than did those subject to production-oriented supervision.

Another programme of research was undertaken at the Personnel Research Board of Ohio State University. The primary aim of this was to develop comprehensive measures of leadership behaviour. From interviews, questionnaires, observation and organizational manuals a 'pool' of some 1,800 statements representing leadership activities in work settings was derived (Stogdill and Shartle, 1948). Experts sorted these statements, and, having eliminated those which overlapped and duplicated one another, arrived at a set of 150 which appeared to represent ten dimensions of leadership behaviour: initiation, representation, fraternization, organization, domination, recognition, production emphasis, integration, communication down, and communication up (Fleishman, 1973). The 150 statements were then incorporated into a questionnaire and administered to large numbers of industrial employees and military personnel. The ten dimensions assumed to exist on the basis of expert judgements were not in practice reflected in the questionnaire responses. Factor analytic techniques showed instead that two major dimensions were sufficient to describe leadership behaviour. These were called *consideration* and *structure*, and were characterized as follows:

Consideration includes behaviour indicating mutual trust, respect, and a certain warmth and rapport between the supervisor and his group . . . This dimension appears to emphasize a deeper concern for group members' needs and includes such behaviour as allowing subordinates more participation in decision-making and encouraging two-way communication.

Structure includes behaviour in which the supervisor organizes and defines group activities and his relation to the group. Thus, he defines the role he expects each member to assume, assigns tasks, plans ahead, establishes ways for getting things done, and pushes for production. This dimension appears to emphasize overt attempts to achieve organizational goals [Fleishman and Harris, 1962].

The concept of consideration is manifestly similar to that of employee-orientation. A more considerate leader is more likely to be influenced by his subordinates and involve them in decision-making than is his less considerate colleague. The relevance of structure to participative leadership is more difficult to establish. It has been shown in many studies to be empirically independent of consideration, so that a participative leader (who is high on consideration) may be high *or* low on structure (Fleishman, 1973). Others have however suggested that a participative style is reflected in high consideration but low structure (Lowin *et al.*, 1969; Blumberg, 1968). It appears that both these interpretations are in part valid. An individual who is extremely high on structure will in practice be low on consideration, but an individual who is moderately high on structure can still emphasize production and organize his subordinates' work in a considerate manner. For our present purposes, however, the more clearly relevant studies deal with consideration, and we shall consequently confine ourselves to these.

Nealey and Blood (1968) found that nurses' satisfaction with their work, supervision, pay and promotion was positively associated with the degree of consideration displayed by their immediate superiors. In two investigations of aircraft commanders (Halpin and Winer, 1957; Halpin, 1957) crew satisfaction was found to be strongly and positively related to consideration. Similar results have been reported by Oaklander and Fleishman (1964) and Seeman (1957). Other evidence indicates that consideration is negatively related to turnover and grievance rates (Fleishman and Harris, 1962; Skinner, 1969). Likert (1961, pp. 16–18) describes findings of a comparable nature. Aspects of supervisory behaviour very similar to the items comprising the consideration measure, such as 'Supervisor takes an interest in me', 'Does some good to discuss important things about my job with supervisor' and 'Supervisor thinks of employees as human beings rather than as persons to get work done', were positively related to favourable work attitudes. And Siegel and Ruh (1973) report similar findings from a study of more than 2,500 employees in six American manufacturing organizations. They found that individuals who judged that they had greater influence over decisions affecting their own jobs also felt more job involvement than did those who perceived less influence (see also Patchen, 1970).

The various investigations, using as they do different measures, and being carried out with employees from many organizations, serve to emphasize the generality of the finding that subordinates who experience greater immediate participation are more satisfied. Moreover, they define more precisely the aspects of leadership which are associated with work satisfaction. We should not, however, be tempted to generalize these results *too* far. The concepts of leadership used have, in most of the studies, involved severely restricted notions of participation. Nowhere is there evidence that employees would be even more satisfied should they be involved on an equal basis with their superiors in decision-making processes. Indeed, the study by Sadler shows that this may not be what employees want. Only 5 and 17 per cent of his respondents, male and female respectively, preferred a superior who accepted a majority viewpoint as a decision. Most wanted to leave the decision-making to their superior with the proviso that he made his judgements in the light of their views.

One further point requires discussion. Dimensions like consideration and employee-orientation incorporate not only the concept of participation, but also aspects of 'niceness' or 'goodness'. On looking at the items, we find that the considerate supervisor 'gets the approval of his foremen on important matters before going ahead', avoids changing 'the duties of people under him without first talking it over with them', 'expresses appreciation when one of us does a good job' and 'is friendly and can be approached' (Fleishman, Harris and Burtt, 1955). He does not 'limit their freedom' (Kahn and Katz, 1953) and 'thinks of employees as human beings' (Likert, 1961). It is not surprising to find that subordinates want their supervisors to display this kind of behaviour, and that they express greater job satisfaction when they perceive it to exist. Most people favour those who, in or out of work, are pleasant to them.

It is even less surprising to find that measures of consideration and job satisfaction are related, since they often include very similar items. One of the most widely used job satisfaction scales is the Job Description Index (Smith, Kendall and Hulin, 1969), and amongst the items in its Supervision Scale we find – 'Asks my advice', 'Praises good work', 'Leaves me on my own' and 'Hard to please'. Hence, whilst the studies have identified some leadership characteristics associated with subordinate satisfaction, the findings are somewhat tautologous. Investigators should thus take it for granted that employees in general will prefer a more 'considerate' style, since this is defined in clearly evaluative terms. The central questions are more difficult: what kinds of people want considerate, employee-oriented, consultative or participative supervisors more than other kinds of people, which employees do not want this style of leadership, and what work circumstances affect the preferences?

During the investigations conducted by the Survey Research Center (see page 92) some instances were encountered where subordinate satisfaction was *not* positively related to the extent to which supervisors were participative. Morse (1953) found clerical employees of an insurance company who worked under more participative supervisors to be no more satisfied with their jobs than those responsible to production-oriented supervisors. The explanation for this apparently inconsistent result focused upon the influence exerted by a supervisor over his or her own superiors. Morse argued that more employee-oriented supervisors encouraged their subordinates to want levels of responsibility and control which, because of the supervisors' relatively restricted powers of influence, could not be met. In this way subordinate expectations raised but not fulfilled counteracted the expected tendency for more participative supervision to encourage job satisfaction.

Pelz (1952) describes some findings with employees of an electricity company which support this argument. Seventy supervisors and their subordinates were involved in the study. The supervisors were divided into two groups, those shown to have considerable influence over their own superiors, and those who had little such influence. The results showed that among those supervisors having considerable influence on their own bosses, subordinate satisfaction was positively related to the supervisor's employee-orientation, but that this was not the case among low-influence supervisors. Pelz summarizes the findings by saying:

> It seems fairly clear, then, that the supervisor's influence or power within the department does 'condition' the way his supervisory behaviour affects employee attitudes. It is plausible to conclude that the supervisory behaviours of 'siding with employees' and 'social closeness to employees' will tend to raise employee satisfaction only if the supervisor has enough influence to make these behaviours pay off in terms of actual benefits for employees [1952, p. 216].

Vroom and Mann (1960) suggest that another factor which mediates the relationship between supervisory style and employee satisfaction is the degree of interaction between supervisor and subordinate. Fifty-two supervisors completed the F-scale (Adorno *et al.*, 1950) which is a measure of authoritarianism (see page 84). In twenty-four small and highly interdependent work-groups, where superior–subordinate interaction was necessarily high, it was found that employees had more positive attitudes towards less authoritarian leaders. In twenty-eight large groups, however, where subordinates were greatly restricted in their interaction with their supervisors, employees had more positive attitudes towards authoritarian leaders. In the latter case the authoritarian leaders provided the necessary control and structure, but because of the job circumstances they left the subordinates to work within that structure.

Vroom (1959) describes related findings indicating that personality characteristics may moderate the relationship between employee participation and satisfaction. 108 supervisors in a large delivery company rated the degree to which they were involved in decision-making. They also indicated their attitudes towards their work and their own superior, and completed two personality scales. One of these was the F-scale, the other a measure of need for independence (adapted from Tannenbaum and Allport, 1956). The relationship between satisfaction and participation for all employees was found to be positive, but it differed according to their personality attributes. For employees who were strongly authoritarian, and for those who had a low need for independence, satisfaction was unrelated to degree of participation. For those with moderate levels of these two personality characteristics, participation and job satisfaction were found to be moderately related. Among non-authoritarian subjects, and those with high independence needs, satisfaction was strongly related to the degree of participation they perceived themselves to have.

In a study involving 488 managers Toshi (1970), applying measures almost identical to those used by Vroom (1959), also observed a strong positive correlation between perceived participation and job satisfaction. However, he failed to replicate Vroom's findings about the moderating function of personality characteristics. The participation–satisfaction relationship remained positive regardless of the authoritarianism or need for independence of the respondents. A study by White and Ruh (1973) also failed to support that of Vroom. The three studies agree that perceived participation and job satisfaction are positively related, but disagree on the relevance of authoritarianism and need for independence as moderators of this relationship.

Research by House (1971) has focused upon the task demands facing an employee. Some jobs are varied and experienced as satisfying in their own right whereas others are limited and felt to require some continuing social support. It appears that in the latter case leader consideration is more strongly associated with subordinate satisfaction than in the former. With less interesting jobs the possibility of some joint decision-making in a friendly atmosphere matters more to a subordinate than it does in conditions of greater self-sufficiency and satisfaction.

These several investigations represent the initial steps towards a more complex view of immediate participation. It is apparent that situational and personal variables can moderate its relationship with work satisfaction; also that there is ample scope for research in this area.

The correlational approach taken by all the projects reviewed so far has the advantage that large numbers of individuals can be studied in their everyday work environments. An important drawback, however, concerns the interpretation of the information obtained. It is tempting to conclude that more participative behaviour on the part of leaders *causes* higher levels of subordinate satisfaction, and that people generally would like more immediate participation than they have at present. Yet it is equally plausible that the reverse may be the case. Employees with more positive work attitudes may well either describe their superiors in more participative terms, or may even evoke more participative behaviour from them. In other words, it is possible that subordinate attitudes determine leadership style rather than the reverse. Lowin and Craig (1968) illustrate this point neatly in relation to subordinate work performance. An experimental research design was used, with forty-eight individuals who were hired for supervisory work in an office. Half of the supervisors were placed in charge of a subordinate who, on the instruction of the investigators, deliberately performed poorly. The other half were responsible for a subordinate with superior work performance. Measures of the closeness of supervision, structure and consideration shown by the supervisors were taken. It was found that the supervisors responsible for subordinates with poor performance adopted closer, more structured and less considerate styles compared with those with subordinates with good work performance. A similar finding is reported by Crowe, Bochner and Clark (1972). Thus subordinate characteristics may determine the behaviour of a leader, and in ongoing organizational situations the pattern is almost bound to be one of mutual influence: leaders affecting subordinates, and subordinates affecting leaders.

Experiments in immediate participation

Experimental research designs in which features of work are manipulated in order to show their relative importance naturally complement the correlational approach. While, for practical reasons, such experiments characteristically involve smaller numbers of subjects, they do more readily permit causal interpretations. The experimental design in the area covered by this chapter involves a deliberate manipulation of the amount of participation in a work situation; the effect of this upon employees' attitudes is then examined.

One of the first studies of this nature was carried out by Coch and French (1948). The setting of the experiment was a pyjama factory, where frequent changes in the production process were necessary to keep abreast of fashion and display requirements. Such changes, involving modifications to work methods and piece rates, were typically accompanied by resistance which manifested itself through high employee turnover, high grievance rates, restriction of output, and aggression towards management. Coch and French decided to investigate participation as a means of introducing new work methods. They selected four groups. The first, the control group, consisted of eighteen employees. In this group the changes were made in the customary manner. The production department studied the new problem, re-designed the work, and set the new piece rates. The group was then informed of the changes. A second group of thirteen employees (referred to as experimental group one) participated through elected representatives. The need for change was explained to the group, and the management presented a plan to involve them, through their representatives, in designing the new work. The remaining two groups, consisting of eight and seven employees, were treated in a comparable fashion to experimental group one, except that group members all participated in making the changes.

The results of the experiment were as follows. The control group showed the customary response to changes in work methods. Three of the group resigned, the remainder were hostile and uncooperative towards their superior and management and complained about the new job. Moreover, there was a deliberate restriction of output which lasted for the forty days of the study. The three experimental groups, in contrast, had no resignations, cooperated with supervision and management, and had unusually high levels of work performance. This was even more marked in the two groups which participated directly than in the group which experienced representational participation. A final change completes the picture. Two and a half months later the remaining members of the control group were again required to change their work methods. On this occasion the modifications were implemented through the direct participative method. This time there was positive response from the group, no labour turnover, full cooperation, and greatly improved work performance. In general the findings suggest that for these employees participation in decision-making led to more positive attitudes towards work as a whole. The absence of direct measures of worker satisfaction, however, makes this conclusion rather tentative.

French was involved in another experiment of this kind (French, Israel and Ås, 1960). A changed manufacturing process was being introduced in a Norwegian shoe factory. Nine four-man groups were selected for study. Of these, four served as control groups, implementing the change in the traditional manner. The other five, experimental, groups participated to a greater extent, determining how the work would be distributed between the groups, what training was required, and how duties would be allocated within their group. The experimental groups expressed greater satisfaction than the control groups on ten out of the fourteen measures used, though in only three instances were the differences statistically significant. Laboratory experiments (for example Bass and Leavitt, 1963) have yielded similar findings.

One of the most extensive field experiments was conducted by Morse and Reimer (1956), in one department of a non-unionized industrial organization. The department had four parallel divisions which employed over 200 women engaged in routine clerical work. For the purposes of investigation the divisions were grouped into pairs which were matched for the degree of participation which existed, the nature of the work, and the satisfaction of the personnel. The design of the experiment involved increasing employee decision-making in one pair of divisions (the autonomy programme) and decreasing it in the other pair (the hierarchically controlled programme). In the autonomy programme authority to make decisions was delegated by upper management to lower levels in the hierarchy where, in turn, it was further delegated to the clerical work-groups. In the hierarchically controlled programme higher level managers were required to increase their influence in running the divisions and to avoid delegating authority to their subordinates. With the cooperation of all levels of management these changes and associated training programmes were introduced over a period of six months and continued for a further year. The success of the programme in changing the level of participation was evaluated. It was clear that the clerks in the autonomy programme felt there had been an increase in participation whilst those in the hierarchically controlled programme were aware of a decrease.

Eight measures were taken of the clerks' satisfaction with management, the company and their jobs. Compared with their attitudes prior to the experiment, those who experienced the autonomy programme showed greater satisfaction on all eight measures, with six of the differences being statistically significant. Moreover, they wanted their programme to continue indefinitely and did not want the alternative system. In contrast, compared with their scores prior to the experiment, those under the hierarchically controlled programme reported lower satisfaction on all eight measures, with six of the differences being statistically significant. They wanted their system to end immediately and to have the autonomy programme instituted in their own divisions. Thus a causal link between participation and various aspects of satisfaction is well illustrated for this population of employees.

Other field experiments, however, have produced less encouraging results. Juralewicz (1974) and Kay, French and Meyer (1962) failed to find any relationship between participation and measures of employee satisfaction. Lawler and Hackman (1969) found that participation in the development of pay incentive plans improved attendance at work. This they explained by suggesting that 'pride in "owning" the plans coupled with an increased trust in management may have enhanced considerably the desire of employees in making the plans a success' (p. 471). However, no evidence from the employees themselves was presented in support of this claim.

Taken together, these experimental studies are no more than *suggestive* of a positive causal relationship between immediate participation and employee satisfaction. Given the widely held belief that such a causal link is well substantiated (see for example Blumberg, 1968, p. 123) it is worth elaborating on the major weaknesses in the available evidence. First, from a purely statistical standpoint, the evidence is unconvincing. Only in the experiment by Morse and Reimer (1956) was there a consistent pattern of statistically significant results showing that the manipulation of participation affected employee satisfaction. French, Israel and Ås (1960) found statistically significant changes on only three out of fourteen measures, and Juralewicz (1974) and Kay, French and Meyer (1962) recorded none at all. In the remaining two field experiments (Coch and French, 1948; Lawler and Hackman, 1969) reliance was placed entirely on the investigators' impressions and there is no guarantee that participants would have described their feelings in the same way. Second, much of the evidence comes from female employees (e.g. Coch and French; Juralewicz; Morse and Reimer; the proportion of males to females in the investigation by French *et al.* is difficult to determine). Finally (with the exception of Morse and Reimer's study) only very small numbers of employees have been involved in these experiments. These last two points reflect upon the relevance of the findings to employees more generally.

Distant participation

The correlational and experimental studies so far considered have concerned immediate participation – the degree of influence exerted by subordinates over decisions directly affecting their own work and made by their immediate superiors. It is also important to discover whether employees gain satisfaction from participation in higher levels of management. This question is particularly pertinent to contemporary discussions in the industrial relations field, which are becoming increasingly concerned with the possibilities for employee participation at all levels within the enterprise.

One of the prerequisites of successful participation is that employees should want to be involved. Walker has called this the 'propensity to participate' (Walker, 1967, 1972). Holter (1965) describes the attitudes towards participation of 1,128 non-supervisory employees of 18 Norwegian organizations. They were asked to say whether, in general, employees participated sufficiently in decisions concerning the management of the organization as a whole. 78 per cent of the blue-collar respondents, and 59 per cent of the white-collar, felt there should be more participation, and only 17 and 37 per cent respectively felt there was already sufficient. The reasons for wanting participation were interesting. Almost 40 per cent felt it would 'increase satisfaction', approximately 25 per cent that it would be 'more just' and about 32 per cent that it would lead to 'greater efficiency'. Holter concludes (1965, p. 290) that there exists 'a widespread, but perhaps vague and diffuse desire for more joint participation in decisions about the firm as a whole'.

Hespe and Little (1971) asked more than 150 non-managerial British employees to indicate the degree of participation they desired for ten situations. Their results are shown in Table 5.4.

The findings complement those of Holter. There is a desire for at least a limited degree of participation in all ten decisions, but this is most wanted in decisions closely associated with everyday work activities (payment methods, work methods, and starting and stopping times).

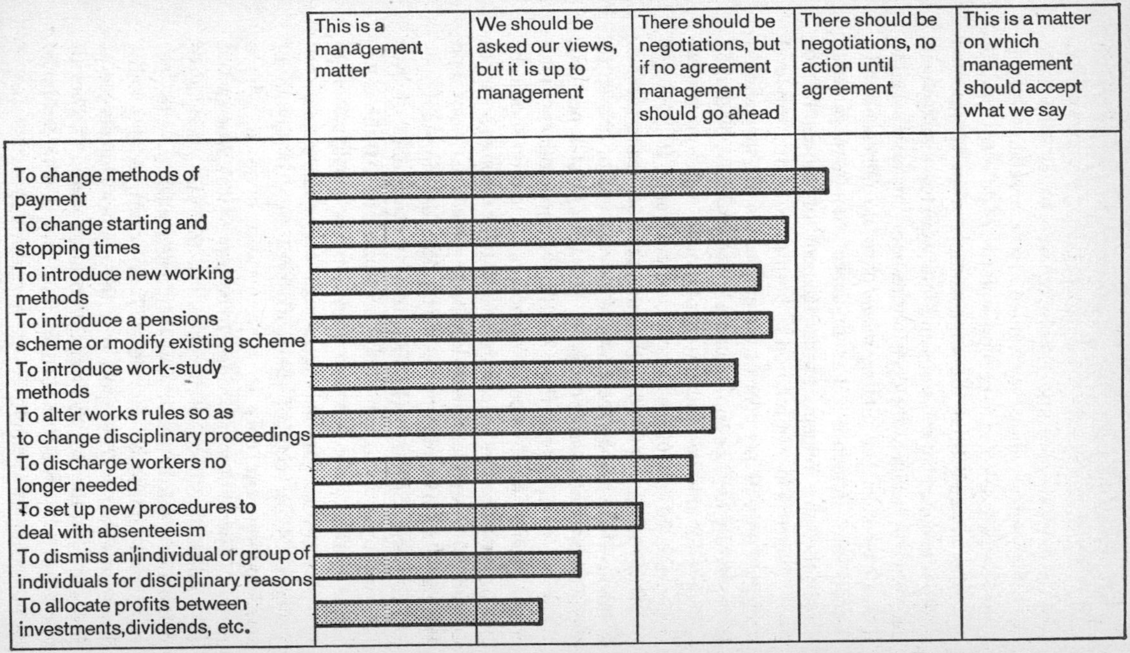

	This is a management matter	We should be asked our views, but it is up to management	There should be negotiations, but if no agreement management should go ahead	There should be negotiations, no action until agreement	This is a matter on which management should accept what we say
To change methods of payment					
To change starting and stopping times					
To introduce new working methods					
To introduce a pensions scheme or modify existing scheme					
To introduce work-study methods					
To alter works rules so as to change disciplinary proceedings					
To discharge workers no longer needed					
To set up new procedures to deal with absenteeism					
To dismiss an individual or group of individuals for disciplinary reasons					
To allocate profits between investments, dividends, etc.					

Table 5.4. The average response of employees from three industrial organizations to a range of decision-making situations

A study of the desire for participation among 127 blue-collar British local authority personnel (Lischeron and Wall, 1975) extends these results. Employees were asked to indicate how much participation they wanted in several separate issues. Each issue was selected to be representative of different kinds of decisions made within the organization. Five represented middle-management decisions and four were top-management decisions. For each of the decisions respondents were asked to indicate whether they felt they *should* have 'no influence at all', 'hardly any influence', 'less influence than management', 'about the same influence as management' or 'more influence than management'. In relation to both middle- and top-level decisions only 21 per cent of the employees felt they should have 'hardly any' or 'no influence'. The majority, 59 and 57 per cent for middle- and top-management decisions respectively, wanted 'about the same as management'. It should be noted, however, that this did not amount to a desire for workers' control, where management would be replaced or chosen by their subordinates, since very few (an average of 8 per cent across the items) felt that they should have 'more influence than management'. Also, when asked how participation should be put into practice, employees preferred it to be through personal contact with superiors in middle-management decisions, and through elected representatives for top-level decision-making.

Tabb and Goldfarb (1970) studied the attitudes of over 850 employees in sixteen Israeli organizations. All the enterprises were designed to encourage worker participation in management decision-making through various representational systems. 54 per cent of the work-force were in favour of participation, and only 16 per cent were opposed, with a further 12 per cent considering it to be impractical. When asked to predict the effects of participation the vast majority of respondents felt it would lead to 'greater efficiency' (84 per cent) and 'improved morale' (77 per cent). Additionally, Brannen *et al.* (1972) report that the majority of people at every level in the British Steel Corporation were in favour of some form of employee participation, and that the majority of non-managerial employees supported the idea of employee directors. Rus (1970) describes seven studies of participation in Yugoslavia and concludes that 'workers tend to feel that the influence of all groups, other than top management, should be increased' (p. 155).

While it is important to ask whether employees want distant participation, it is also relevant to discover how they respond to its existence. Several authors have suggested that organizations which allow little opportunity for distant participation tend to have employees with less positive work attitudes. Blauner (1964) found that employees in low-participation organizations experienced a sense of powerlessness, and Pearlin (1962) observed that lack of participation was related to job dissatisfaction among nursing personnel. A study by Aiken and Hage (1966) in sixteen American welfare agencies led to similar conclusions. Etzioni (1964), however, has proposed that participation is more likely to be related to job attitudes among professional employees than among others. This suggestion is supported by several studies which have found level of education to be positively related to attitudes towards participation (Sadler, 1966; Tabb and Goldfarb, 1970). However, Lischeron and Wall (1975) found that perceived distant participation was positively associated with job satisfaction even among blue-collar employees with limited education.

To impose causal interpretations on correlational evidence of this nature is a dubious exercise (see page 99). There is no adequate alternative to an experimental investigation if one wishes to establish whether employee participation in higher levels of management decision-making is a determinant of more positive work attitudes. One such experiment is reported by Lischeron and Wall (1976). They implemented a participative system, based upon regular meetings between small groups of employees and managers, which was designed to increase employees' influence in decisions made at middle- and top-management level. The system was run for a trial period of five months with an experimental group of 150 workpeople and a control group of 200 employees who were not afforded the opportunity to participate.

Over 90 per cent of the employees in the experimental group voluntarily attended all of the meetings. At the end of the trial period it was clear that experimental subjects, compared to their control-group counterparts, felt they were more involved and had greater influence in management decision-making. Moreover, they were strongly in favour of the participative system itself. Some 91 per cent of the experimental employees recommended the continuation of the system and its extension to the control group. Employees in the experimental group also demonstrated more positive attitudes towards middle management. There were, however, no changes in attitudes towards broader features of the working environment; satisfaction with the organization as a whole, the work itself, immediate supervisors and opportunities for promotion remained unaffected. In other words, whilst participation had been increased, and had been favourably received by employees, it did not result in wide-ranging or fundamentally improved attitudes towards their total work situation. There was nevertheless sufficient change for the organization in question to accept the verdict of its employees and extend the participation scheme to other groups.

In contrast to the relatively informal voluntary approach described above, participative systems have been imposed in many countries by political action. In Yugoslavia, for instance, participation has been legally required through the medium of workers' councils. These councils, consisting of fifteen to 120 members, depending upon the size of the organization, are given the legal responsibility for determining the overall activities of the enterprise. They elect and supervise their own executive committees, appoint the directors of their organization, and examine their boards' reports. Shop-floor personnel comprise the large majority of council members. It is extremely difficult to assess the effect of this system upon the attitudes and well-being of the workers involved since the changes are so wide-ranging and are continually being modified. Blumberg (1968) takes an optimistic view, though the majority of commentators tend to regard the system as providing little real involvement for shop-floor personnel and as being of only tangential relevance to their attitudes towards work. Kolaja (1961, 1965), for instance, analysed the contributions in workers' council meetings made by management and non-management personnel and observed that the former still monopolized the decision-making. Broekmeyer (1968) also conducted a study of this form of participation and observed restricted support among employees. When reactions were invited about proposals on very important questions there was no response from the shop floor; and, in spite of the large number of employee representatives, 90 per cent of the discussion in the councils emanated from the minority of specialists, managers and those with higher education. Similar findings are reported by Rosenstein (1970) about the Israeli programme for distant participation. In this investigation, four different attempts to give employee representatives formal channels through which they could legitimately influence higher-management decision-making were seen as unsuccessful. Rosenstein (1970, p. 181) concludes that 'the activities of the worker-directors have failed to promote a feeling of satisfaction among the rank and file. The hope that a programme would cause an improvement in the work atmosphere in the enterprise, or that it would cause workers to identify more with their work place, has not materialized'.

Tannenbaum *et al.* (1974) compared the views of workers in Yugoslav industry and in the Israeli kibbutz system with the attitudes of Italian, Austrian and American workers. They found that whilst the Yugoslav and Israeli organizations 'may not function entirely according to ideological prescriptions' (p. 23) they nevertheless were seen by their employees as participative. In other words employees in Yugoslavia and in kibbutz plants in Israel reported higher levels of participation than did their counterparts in Italy, Austria and the United States. These differences in participation were not reflected, however, in variations in work satisfaction, trust, sense of responsibility and work motivation. Whilst employees in the kibbutz were typically high on these dimensions, those from Yugoslavia fell below those from the less participative enterprises in America. Even from such large-scale comparisons it is clear that the relationship between participation and well-being is highly complex.

West Germany operates works councils consisting of members elected by all employees regardless of union membership. Those more than eighteen years old and with more than six months' service are eligible to vote or to be elected. The size of the council is related to the number of employees it represents. The works council has the legal right to equal influence with the employers in several decision-making areas as well as a right to the supply of adequate information from management about impending decisions. A helpful account of the nature and powers of these works councils, and a consideration of their relevance to British industrial relations, is provided by Roberts (1973). Employees' attitudes towards this system of representation are strongly favourable. This is evidenced not only by the fact that between 50 and 90 per cent of employees express approval of works councils and believe them to be important to them individually, but also that up to 88 per cent participate in council elections (Roberts, 1973, pp. 354–6).

Emery and Thorsrud (1969) looked at employee representatives on company boards of directors in five Norwegian companies. They found that these individuals played only a restricted role in the decision-making processes, largely because of their lack of expert knowledge of the issues under discussion. Additionally, the extent to which they were representative was questionable since there was little evidence of feedback and communication with their electors.

In the United Kingdom there has developed a particularly sharp distinction between 'negotiation' and 'consultation'. These are both processes through which employees influence the organization's decisions, but their content and machinery are traditionally quite separate. Negotiation takes place over wages and conditions of work; and all other management–worker issues are typically discussed through consultation. The essence of negotiation is that management may not introduce changes until agreement has been reached; unilateral alterations to hours of work or wage levels are thus not acceptable.

Consultative processes, on the other hand, leave the final decision in the hands of management.

In all but the smallest companies, negotiations of any importance will involve one or more trade unions, and there are several factors which lead unions to emphasize negotiating procedures at the expense of consultation. In the first place negotiations give trade unionists more power. Secondly, they deal with tangible and clearly important issues. Negotiations have also been the traditional mechanism through which the trade union movement has made its presence felt, not only to management but also amongst potential members and the public at large. Recent attempts by government to inhibit freedom in collective bargaining have resulted in deeply felt reactions from the unions.

The past decades have seen a steady increase in the amount and scope of union–management negotiation. We need not ask whether union members are in favour of this development: obviously they are. It is the extension of consultative procedures with which we are concerned here. The majority of medium-size and large organizations in the United Kingdom have some network of what are known as consultative committees, works committees or works councils. These are usually thought of as attempts to foster distant participation, yet there exists a widespread feeling among both sides of industry that they are of only moderate value. In part this arises from their perceived lower status relative to negotiation, and in part it is a reaction to the topics which are discussed. These must by definition be of general interest to all committee members (so that specific issues are discussed outside the joint consultative system) but must exclude pay and conditions (which are subject to negotiation). In practice then, many consultative committees spend a great deal of time discussing minor issues such as the cleanliness of the canteen or the toilets. Employee attendance at this type of meeting is often somewhat reluctant.

This point may be illustrated through these comments from a junior manager describing the works council in his factory:

When I heard that I had been appointed to this for a year I was delighted. But disillusionment set in after a few months because of all the paltry, pettifogging matters we discussed: when would there be new gates on the company houses, should steel-toe-capped safety shoes be allowed out of the works if the men had actually bought them, what about moving the bus stop a few yards nearer, should men on hot plants have lime-juice or salt tablets, or a mixture of them. The works manager took the chair, the labour officer was secretary. There were councillors from the payroll staff in each department, some of whom were shop stewards though the majority were not. One councillor who had least to say at council meetings was a senior shop steward of the Amalgamated Engineering Union. He merely sat there with a cynical expression on his face. I think the one thing he and the works manager had in common was that they both knew what the company's idea was in having the works council. Afterwards we always had a ham and chips tea on the company before dispersing to go home about 6.30 [Fraser, 1969, pp. 183–4].

Another difficulty sometimes attached to consultative committees arises from their need to be made up of elected representatives of the employees as a whole. How should such elections take place? In a large plant any choice of a small number of representatives must leave many employees with the feeling that they are to all intents and purposes excluded from the consultative process. But beyond this, should the electors or the representatives be restricted to trade union members? In some companies where only a moderate proportion of employees belong to trade unions these questions can generate sufficient conflict to bring the whole idea of consultative mechanisms into severe doubt. In other plants, perhaps where union membership is higher, there may still be problems attached to the ratio of representatives from each major union or employee group.

It is apparent, therefore, that distant participation through representative procedures is not without its difficulties. Such procedures may remain necessary where no alternatives are possible, and there are undoubtedly instances of successful consultation. In most cases, however, they are of very limited concern to the average employee. In an account of developments within the Glacier Metal Company, Jaques (1951, p. 132) reports that 'employees were generally uninterested in, or apathetic to, the joint consultative bodies', and Emery and Thorsrud (1969, p. 58) found 'no evidence of a change in the attitudes of the rank and file either in respect of the representative structure or in respect of their involvement in the work of the company'. Distant participation may thus be important as a kind of safety-net. Employees may like to know that procedures exist, even if they use them relatively infrequently and if their day-to-day lives are not materially affected by them. The parallel here with parliamentary democracy in society more generally is a strong one.

Overview

In this chapter we have distinguished between immediate and distant participation. Immediate participation is a matter of face-to-face interaction between an individual and his own supervisor on job-related issues, whereas distant participation typically involves meetings among groups of representatives from management and workers and deals with matters of more general relevance. We have documented the extensive evidence that people want immediate participation and that increases in this respect can enhance their well-being at work. The need to extend research into the significance of personal and situational variations has been stressed (cf. Heller, 1973; House, 1971; Vroom, 1959; White and Ruh, 1973). We have also indicated that many employees tend to value increased distant participation. On the other hand, they are less concerned about distant than about immediate issues, and Strauss and Rosenstein's conclusion (1970, p. 213) is generally applicable:

> Jobs, supervision styles and even methods of compensation must be redesigned to permit workers a sense of autonomy and achievement in their daily work. In other words, for formal representative participation to work, it may be necessary to first introduce informal, human relations style participation on the job.

Before leaving these questions of participation and well-being we should, however, ask, 'Whose well-being is at stake?' The discussion throughout the chapter has been in terms of subordinate attitudes and we started by noting how psychologists fifty years ago had already recognized workers' demands for greater influence. Changes have been made in the intervening years, but their limited extent requires explanation as much as the fact that they have occurred. In brief it may be noted that managerial well-being is often threatened by increasing employee influence.

It is clear that a manager who is empowered to reach his own decisions and who can expect his instructions to be obeyed by subordinates is fairly comfortably placed. He can devote his attention to improving his plant, training his employees, planning ahead and setting up procedures and operations. He will meet difficulties and be subject to pressures of various kinds, but at least he knows that he is free to make decisions and that these will be carried out. Such an unambiguous position is relatively free from anxiety.

It has in fact been the traditional 'tells' or 'sells' style of management (see page 88) that has predominated in work organizations. The manager who is asked to adopt a more consultative approach loses his 'status congruence' (see page 73) and soon experiences greater stress and anxiety. In part this arises from the increased ambiguity which is generated: which of his plans will prove acceptable? It also comes from the fact that he needs so much more time for meetings and that people who need to be consulted may not be immediately available. In times of pressure decisions thus have to be deferred; prolonged uncertainty over important issues is associated with anxiety and discomfort. The process of discussion in order to reach agreement may well open up conflicts among colleagues and between managers and their subordinates; not everyone's view can be acted upon, and as discussion proceeds small conflicts can easily lead to larger ones.

The participative manager has lost the simple life of the 'tells' manager. He has to be able to operate within a shifting environment which lacks certainty and clear predictability. His own ability is constantly in question: not only do people disagree with proposals to which he is personally committed, but quite often they substitute others which he sees to be better than those he was himself able to produce. In an atmosphere of constant questioning, union–management relations will from time to time hit a particularly sticky patch. His management colleagues will ask for 'strong leadership to show the workers who runs the plant'. The surface attraction of such a response will possibly add to his mental conflict: can he really trust his employees, do they have his well-being in mind in the same way that he is asked to consider theirs?

It is the essence of any relationship, at work and elsewhere, that one person's freedom to do as he wants is constrained by the other person. Subordinates' wishes for increased participation conflict with superiors' preferences for straightforward decision-making procedures based upon their own authority. Such conflicts seem to be inherent in any kind of organizational decision-making and studies of their operation are still needed. The bulk of research so far has focused merely upon the attitudes of subordinates. Future progress may be greater if research shows a simultaneous concern with both parties' wants and with practical experiments into their reconciliation.

6 Designing jobs for people

The studies of immediate participation reviewed in the previous chapter concerned the extent to which an employee's freedom of action was constrained by his supervisor. A related question is how far his freedom is constrained by the content of the job itself. Many jobs, especially those in the manufacturing industry, are extremely narrow and specialized. The movement towards work simplification has largely been a deliberate process, as a study by Davis, Canter and Hoffman (1955) illustrates. Personnel concerned with organizing work for shop-floor employees in twenty-four American industrial companies rated fourteen factors for their importance to job design. Their replies are shown in Table 6.1.

As the authors conclude, 'the majority of companies believed in limiting the content of individual jobs as much as possible. This means limiting the number of tasks within jobs and limiting the variations permitted in tasks or jobs' (p. 7). Factors relevant to employee well-being emerge as quite unimportant in these operational decisions.

Few would deny the economic success associated with this approach to job design, the prime example of which is the assembly line. The rationale is relatively straightforward. If jobs are simplified, monetary costs are reduced, since errors are less likely to occur, less-skilled labour may be recruited, and training times are shortened. Scientific management approaches (see pages 24 to 27), work study and ergonomics have all played their part in encouraging work simplification. In its most extreme form a simplified job may be characterized for the individual by: the continuous repetition of a single operation with a short time-cycle, no discretion over how to carry out the tasks, no control over the pace of work, and,

Table 6.1. Major factors in choice of particular methods for performing operations

Factor	*Total number of times mentioned in order of importance from high (5) to low (1)*					*Weighted rating*
	(5)	(4)	(3)	(2)	(1)	
Minimizing time required to perform operation	14	4	1	—	—	89
Obtaining highest quality possible	4	6	1	3	—	53
Minimizing skill requirements of operation	1	3	4	3	4	39
Use of equipment or tools presently on hand	1	4	2	—	—	27
Minimizing floor-space requirements	2	2	1	1	—	23
Achieving specialization of skills	—	1	4	1	1	19
Minimizing learning time or training	—	—	4	—	1	13
Minimizing materials-handling costs	1	—	—	2	1	10
Equalizing and developing full work-load	—	1	1	1	—	9
Providing operator satisfaction	—	1	1	1	—	9
Minimizing equipment and tool costs	—	1	—	1	1	7
Controlling materials used in operation	—	—	1	2	—	7
Providing maximum production flexibility	—	1	1	—	—	7
Simplifying supervision of operation	—	—	—	—	3	3
Providing maximum safety in operation	—	—	—	1	1	3

perhaps as an unintended consequence, severely restricted opportunities for social interaction in the work situation.

Attitudinal correlates of work simplification

While the practice of work simplification may be justified on economic grounds, many would oppose it for its effect on employees' well-being. It has often been argued that as jobs become increasingly repetitive, routine and broken-up, they can only have detrimental effects upon the satisfaction and mental health of job-holders. Such a theme underlies many of the ideas discussed in the first chapter, and we shall examine here the evidence which has been gathered about it.

People's descriptions of their own jobs often focus upon their feelings towards the repetitive nature of their work. Consider the following verbatim account from an employee in a chemical process plant:

> If I thought there was no hope of ever having more variety than continuously running out batches and cleaning jobs, but to stand under a blender in one position, day after day, just opening and shutting the valve, it's not my idea of satisfactory. Though, as they say, somebody has to do it, but I don't see why it should be me [Wall, 1971, p. 252].

A written account from an employee in a cigarette factory repeats the feelings rather more grammatically.

> In the industry in which I work the worker's role is becoming more and more that of an onlooker and less that of a participant. Mechanization, though it has played a part in the achievement of a shorter working week, has led to jobs that are both dull and monotonous. The loss of dignity and restriction of talent compatible with modern factory life cause a lack of quality in the factory worker [Fraser, 1968, p. 16].

Clerical staff often report the same reactions:

> One occupational hazard facing a clerk is always the sense of futility he struggles against, or is more often just overwhelmed by. Unlike even the humblest worker on a production line, he doesn't produce *anything*. He battles with phantoms, abstracts: runs in a paper chase that goes on year after year, and seems utterly pointless.

How can there be anything else other than boredom in it for him? [Fraser, 1968, pp. 57–8].

The psychological consequence of repetitive work is not a new theme. The Medical Research Council's Industrial Fatigue Board was responsible for much of the early empirical research on this question. These early studies involved intensive observation of small groups of British employees engaged in highly repetitive work, such as pharmaceutical product packaging (Wyatt and Ogden, 1924), soap wrapping, handkerchief folding, bicycle-chain assembly, tobacco-weighing, cigarette-making, cartridge-case assembly (Wyatt, Fraser and Stock, 1928) and sewing (Burnett, 1925). The work performance and attitudes of employees were recorded under standard working conditions and also after changes had been introduced in order to increase the variety of operations. The results suggested that a certain degree of increase in variety improved output, though too much had adverse effects since it broke up the work rhythm of the operators. However, employees responded favourably to increased variety. As Wyatt, Fraser and Stock (1928, p. 25) report, 'operatives who have had experience of both uniform and varied conditions of work generally prefer the latter'.

A subsequent Industrial Health Board inquiry (Fraser, 1947) was concerned with the incidence of neurotic illness among more than 3,000 male and female employees in thirteen British light- and medium-engineering factories. The occurrence of neurosis during a six-month period was examined in relation to personal characteristics of employees, social-background variables, and work-environment factors. Age and intelligence were found to have little association with neurosis, as were type of house and district of residence. Work factors, however, did emerge as being important. Neurotic illness was most common among those who found work boring, held a job offering little variety, were engaged in assembly, bench inspection or toolroom work, or performed jobs requiring constant attention. Fraser summarized the findings as follows: 'It may be less important to make jobs "foolproof" than to design them so that they will not be disliked, found boring, or demand long periods of close attention to unvarying detail . . . More variety, and scope for initiative and interest could be introduced without any fundamental alteration of production programmes' (1947, p. 10).

Walker and Guest (1952) investigated the relationship between repetitiveness in assembly-line work and job attitudes in American car workers. Repetitiveness was measured by the number of different operations carried out by the individual. Of those performing more than five operations, 69 per cent found their jobs fairly or very interesting. Of those performing two to five operations, 44 per cent gave the same response, whilst of those whose job involved a single operation only 33 per cent felt their work to be fairly or very interesting. Many individuals, particularly those on jobs involving fewest operations, complained of the repetitive and monotonous nature of their work.

Comparable conclusions have been reached on the basis of more recent studies. Shepard (1969) examined the attitudes of employees engaged in three types of work: mechanized production jobs where 'minute subdivision of operations is at its height', automated production systems where simplification is less extreme, and craft production systems where considerably more variety is in evidence. The results showed a strong relationship between job satisfaction and degree of specialization as represented by the three job types. 86 per cent of the mechanized production employees reported low overall job satisfaction, whereas the proportions for automated production employees and craftsmen were 48 and 13 per cent respectively. In other words, the least satisfied individuals were to be found engaged in work which involved the greatest specialization and least variety. Additionally, those in the more simplified jobs were more likely to see their work as meaningless, to feel a sense of powerlessness, and experience a lack of autonomy; this is 'alienation' in the classic sense (see page 22). Unfortunately, Shepard does not report the relationship between job satisfaction and other factors which might have varied systematically across the three jobs (for example, pay and work conditions), so it is not clear to what extent the observed attitudinal differences are solely related to job-content factors and to what extent they might be accounted for by other variables.

This problem was to some extent overcome in a study by Kornhauser (1965). He assessed the mental health of more than 400 male blue-collar employees in thirteen Detroit car factories. Mental health was defined as a positive orientation to life evidenced by low anxiety and tension, high self-esteem, trust rather than hostility towards others, sociability as opposed to withdrawal, high satisfaction with life and high personal morale as opposed to despair. Mental health was found to be highest among those in more skilled work, and lowest for those engaged in repetitive, routine, machine-paced, semi-skilled jobs. The analysis did not stop there, but included consideration of several dimensions which varied across the different job types in an attempt to uncover those factors most closely associated with mental health. For example, level of education was positively related to both job level and mental health. However, within sub-populations with equal levels of education, mental health was still higher among those individuals performing more skilled work. Similarly, variations in perceived job security, satisfaction with pay, work conditions, promotional opportunities, interpersonal relations, and family background characteristics did not account for the observed mental health differences. In contrast, job satisfaction and the extent to which individuals saw their work as giving them the chance to use their abilities were consistently important correlates of psychological health. Kornhauser concludes (1965, p. 363) that 'by far the most influential attribute [of jobs] is the opportunity work offers – or fails to offer – for use of the worker's abilities and for associated feelings of interest, sense of accomplishment, personal growth and self-respect'. Repetitive, routine jobs were seen as offering few such opportunities.

Whilst this study is very thorough in many ways, it still leaves much unanswered. The causal relationship of mental health to different job characteristics is truly complex. We cannot tell whether it is the nature of jobs which causes superior or inferior mental health, or whether those less well adjusted to life opt for jobs which they consider to be less demanding, that is jobs which, by virtue of being repetitive and routine, are more predictable and may consequently be seen as less stressful. We would need to discover, for instance, whether individuals transferred from more repetitive to more challenging work demonstrated improvements in mental health, and vice versa. To our knowledge, for practical and ethical reasons, such manipulations have not been undertaken and investigated. Furthermore, we should not forget that any assessment of mental health is based upon a value system, and that the values involved are more likely to be compatible with those of the individuals in more skilled jobs. Both these points are equally relevant to the study by Fraser (1947) described on page 119.

The relationship between job content variables and individual attitudes was also investigated by Hackman and Lawler (1971). Thirteen different jobs, carried out by 208 employees in an American telephone company, were examined and described in terms of the following four variables.

(i) *variety:* the degree to which the job required employees to perform a wide range of operations and/or the degree to which employees had to use a variety of equipment and procedures;

(ii) *autonomy:* the extent to which employees had a major say in organizing their work, choosing the equipment they would use, and selecting the procedures to be followed;

(iii) *task identity:* the extent to which employees did an entire piece of work and could identify the result of their own efforts;

(iv) *feedback:* the degree to which individuals received information concerning their performance.

The jobs were classified in terms of these four features, and several measures of employee attitudes about their work were also taken. The relationships between the job-content variables and a selection of the attitude measures are shown in Table 6.2, which is adapted from Hackman and Lawler (1971, p. 273).

Table 6.2. Product–moment correlation coefficients for the relationship between job-content variables and employee attitudes and performance

	Job-content variables			
Employee attitude measures	*Variety*	*Autonomy*	*Task identity*	*Feedback*
Overall job satisfaction	0·38	0·39	0·20	0·28
Job involvement	0·24	0·22	0·12	0·24
Self-esteem from job	0·32	0·32	0·15	0·35
Feeling of worthwhile accomplishment	0·29	0·32	0·28	0·42
Respect and fair treatment from boss	0·19	0·26	0·22	0·35
Personal growth and development	0·36	0·34	0·14	0·31
Prestige of job inside company	0·30	0·25	0·15	0·35
Pay	0·04	0·05	0·04	0·34

(Correlations above 0·11 are significant beyond the 5 per cent level by a one-tailed test.)

Correlation coefficients can vary between −1·00 and +1·00. The nearer the coefficient is to 1·00, the stronger the relationship between the two variables measured. Thus the correlation of 0·38 between variety and overall job satisfaction shown in Table 6.2 indicates that the greater the variety involved in a job, the greater is the overall satisfaction reported by individual holders of that job. In general, it can be seen that there are consistent positive relationships between each of the four job-content variables and the measures of employee attitudes. This is to say that individuals in jobs offering greater variety, autonomy, task identity and feedback tend to exhibit more positive work attitudes. The fact that attitude towards pay is unrelated to three of the job characteristics weighs against the interpretation that as pay varies systematically with nature of work it is the cause of the observed relationships.

Evidence of this nature has led many (for example Argyris, 1957, 1964; Blauner, 1964; Davis, 1957; Kornhauser, 1965; Likert, 1961; McGregor, 1957; Whyte, 1955) to the conclusion that job simplification leads almost inevitably to monotony, boredom and job dissatisfaction. Whilst this is one plausible interpretation of the findings and the conclusion usually reached, there are alternative explanations. No one study can be definitive, and each investigation is interpretable in several different ways. Thus we must register the possibility that the observed differences in attitudes and mental health between incumbents of more and less repetitive jobs may be attributable to other factors, or combinations of circumstances, which vary systematically with degree of repetitiveness. Moreover, we cannot reject the possibility that some individuals are predisposed towards dissatisfaction or mental illness and also opt for more repetitive work.

Several investigators have also questioned the generality of the conclusion that simplified jobs *cause* negative work attitudes. Some have suggested that we have witnessed 'ethnomorphizing' in this area of research (Hulin and Blood, 1968; Hulin, 1971). This is to say that social scientists have overstated the case by attributing to all members of society values and desires which in reality are only characteristic of their own middle-class sub-culture. Certainly, the fact that different groups of employees value different features of the work environment is well documented (for example, Centers and Bugental, 1966; Friedlander, 1965). Higher-level employees place greater emphasis upon the nature of their work, whilst their lower-level counterparts stress pay, security and fringe benefits. Further evidence comes from a study by Turner and Lawrence (1965), who have proposed that the cultural background of employees moderates their attitude towards job-content factors. They found that employees in factories situated in small towns exhibited positive attitudes when their jobs offered greater variety, were more complex and involved greater responsibility. This was not the case, however, with employees from more urbanized environments where satisfaction was lower among those holding jobs which involved greater variety and less repetition. Turner and Lawrence attempted to explain this difference by arguing that blue-collar employees in large cities would be more likely to reject white-collar values (which stress the importance of autonomy, responsibility and challenging work) than would their peers in more rural environments. City workers would consequently be less likely to see these aspects as sources of satisfaction. Blood and Hulin (1967) report similar results as does Wild (1970), who found that 'workers in more urban areas are better disposed to accepting or tolerating the rationalized unskilled and paced manual jobs commonly found in industry' (p. 45).

Hackman and Lawler (1971) adopted an alternative strategy for examining the same issue. Rather than taking into account cultural differences, they measured individuals' values with respect to 'higher-order needs' such as desire for autonomy, challenge, variety and opportunity for achievement (these values they saw as more compatible with 'integrated', or small-town, cultures). They then compared groups with strong or less strong 'higher-order needs'. The results indicated a more marked positive relationship between work attitudes and the existence of variety, autonomy, task identity and feedback for the group with stronger 'higher-order needs' than for the group which exhibited weaker needs, but the relationship was positive in *both* cases.

A recent study by Susman (1973), however, showed that employees from both rural and urban backgrounds responded favourably towards more varied and responsible jobs. This calls into question whether values (measured at a sub-cultural or an individual level) necessarily moderate the relationship between job content and repetitiveness and work satisfaction. We should also note that the geographical and social differences between urban and rural communities in the USA (where most of the studies have been conducted) far exceed the differences in Britain and other smaller countries. Nevertheless individual differences are clearly relevant. Married women working part-time quite often value the financial and social rewards from their job more than the opportunity for challenge. More generally, Smith (1955) has shown that great variations exist between employees with respect to their susceptibility to monotony. Studies by Kennedy and O'Neill (1958) and Kilbridge (1960) also suggest that among blue-collar employees more varied jobs may not always be preferred nor result in improved job satisfaction. It thus seems clear that there is a proportion of the work-force to whom a job offering greater variety, challenge and responsibility may not be an attractive prospect: a key issue concerns the characterization of this group, and more research is urgently needed. Yet, there is sufficient evidence that many individuals at present carrying out highly repetitive work would respond favourably to more varied and complex jobs, and that such jobs would be important contributors to their positive mental health as described in Chapter 1. Let us therefore consider some ways in which these changes might be made.

Proposals for re-designing simplified jobs

There have been several proposals about how to organize work in order to avoid the consequences of simplification whilst at the same time allowing the economic goals of the enterprise to be attained. These range from minor modifications to existing jobs to comparatively major changes in the social and technological work environment. They have been put into practice in such diverse occupations as domestic cleaning, assembly-line work, clerical work and selling. The terms most commonly used to denote the different ideas are job rotation, horizontal job enlargement, job extension, vertical job enlargement, job enrichment and autonomous working-groups. It is appropriate to consider the meanings of these different terms and their interrelationships before going on to evaluate the effects of their implementation upon employee attitudes.

One of the earliest suggestions was that of *job rotation*. The principle behind job rotation is to increase the variety of operations performed by the individual through allowing him to move, perhaps at specified intervals, from one job to another. Whilst this does not affect the content of any single job, and consequently the basic work-processes remain undisturbed, it does increase the range of activities experienced by the employee. The cost to the employing organization is the need to train individuals in more than one job, though this may be offset by greater flexibility in the allocation of labour. It will be appreciated that job rotation is quite common in work organizations: in one cannery with which we are familiar two groups of operators exchange their repetitive jobs half-way through a shift; neither they nor their superiors see anything experimental or unusual in this. Thus job rotation often exists in practice even though it may not be formally identified as such.

The aim of *horizontal job enlargement* is the same, to increase the variety of tasks. The difference is that this is achieved by changing the job content in order to include a larger number of differing tasks, rather than by moving the individual between jobs. It is, however, to be distinguished from *job extension*, defined as the addition of more very similar tasks, which increases the number but not markedly the variety of operations performed by the individual.

Whereas the first three ways of changing the design of jobs all operate upon the range of tasks involved, the remainder focus more upon the discretionary element of work. *Vertical job enlargement* refers to an increase in the degree to which an individual can control the planning and execution of his work. Thus he may be given greater discretion over how to set about his task and how to organize his time. *Job enrichment* is an alternative term for vertical job enlargement. The use of a separate expression reflects principally a difference in theoretical origins. Whilst vertical job enlargement is unrelated to any one particular theoretical orientation, job enrichment has evolved in close association with Herzberg's two-factor theory of work motivation (see Chapter 2, page 35). It has been defined as 'building into people's jobs, quite specifically, greater scope for personal achievement and recognition, more challenging and responsible work, and more opportunity for advancement and growth' (Paul and Robertson, 1970, p. 17). This reflects the work attributes stressed by the two-factor theory as being of crucial importance to employee satisfaction and mental health. In practice job-enrichment programmes involve increased responsibility for the job-holder along the lines used in vertical job-enlargement programmes.

The idea of *autonomous working-groups* has a rather wider conceptual basis. It emphasizes not only increased discretion for the employee, but also that this should be provided on a group basis. Davis and Taylor (1972, pp. 17–18) offer the following definition: 'Autonomous groups are effectively leaderless teams of employees working together in the completion of the group's primary task.' Davis (1966) further describes autonomous behaviour as '(a) self-regulation of work content and structure within the job . . ., (b) self-evaluation of performance, (c) self-adjustment to changes required by technological variability, and (d) participation in setting up goals or objectives for job outputs'. The overall aim of autonomous working-groups is to provide a job which is complete in the sense that the group sees it through from beginning to end and also has the responsibility for planning, coordinating and evaluating its own work activities, within broad constraints reached through the participation of the group members in joint decision-making with their superiors.

In principle we should be able to implement these six forms of job design, determine the relative merits of each, and identify the specific changes to the organization of work which contribute, or fail to contribute, to employee well-being. In practice, however, this is not feasible, for two reasons. First, there is considerable overlap between the various approaches with respect to the changes in the work situation required for their implementation. For example, vertical job enlargement (or job enrichment) provides greater discretion for the employee in carrying out his work. As a result the individual is free within agreed limits to vary his activities from time to time; he may change the order in which he carries out his various tasks, and he may even take on additional tasks. Thus while he has more responsibility, he may also be instituting his own 'job rotation' or 'horizontal job enlargement'. Similar overlap may also occur as a result of the introduction of autonomous working-groups, where as a result of increased group discretion greater variety of activities and increased discretion may fall upon the shoulders of the individual. Thus in introducing one form of job design, changes are often made which correspond to those emphasized by another. Second, the implementation of any one form of job design typically involves simultaneous modifications to a wide range of different features of the work environment. Increasing the employee's responsibility for his own work, for instance, alters the role of the immediate superior and may change the relationship between the subordinate and his superior. Similarly, to enable autonomous working-groups to organize their work effectively, it may be necessary to change their payment system or to provide them with new functions such as requisitioning supplies and raw materials.

Taking a wider perspective, it will be recognized that on a practical level not only do the different approaches interrelate and involve simultaneous changes across a broad spectrum of work factors, but they also overlap with areas of research which are traditionally labelled differently. Job enrichment and vertical enlargement programmes will often be indistinguishable from experiments in immediate participation (see Chapter 5); and changes to the social composition of work-groups (see Chapter 4) bear closely upon the changes central to the notion of autonomous working-groups. Hence the modifications required by the different types of job design carry over across the conceptual boundaries between them, and also spread into other areas of research. Whilst this may be unfortunate in preventing a tidy analysis of separate variables, it is inherent in the subject-matter. And it is still possible to evaluate the effects of the composite changes introduced under the banner of any one of the approaches described. Indeed, it is debatable whether it is desirable to attempt to isolate the effects of any one component of change in circumstances where changes cannot themselves readily be made in isolation. What is important is whether or not the total pattern of changes affects the well-being of individuals. Bearing these points in mind let us examine attempts that have been made to re-design jobs to include greater variety and discretion.

Experiments with re-designed jobs

Some early case-studies of job enlargement are reported by Biggane and Stewart (1963). One study concerned a change in the jobs of employees producing top-covers for washing-machines. The covers consisted of forty-six sub-components which, prior to the enlargement programme, were assembled by groups of operators working from conveyor-belts. The cycle time for each group under this arrangement was approximately half a minute, and quality control was carried out when the whole washing-machine had been completed. The job was modified so that each operator was individually responsible for the assembly *and* inspection of a complete top-cover. The resultant cycle time was approximately nine minutes. Thus the enlargement of this job involved several changes, the principal ones being increased variety of operations, additional responsibility in relation to the inspection of the work carried out, increased control over the pace of work, and responsibility for the assembly of a relatively complete end-product. Unfortunately the effects of these changes on employee attitudes were not systematically investigated, and no statistical evidence was reported. Nevertheless, observation of this experiment, and of fourteen others, led Biggane and Stewart to the conclusion that 'a large majority of operators came to prefer job enlargement in a relatively short time', that labour costs were lower, and quality of work improved.

Paul, Robertson and Herzberg (1969) and Paul and Robertson (1970) describe the effects of job enrichment applied to the work of sales representatives, design engineers, factory supervisors and laboratory technicians. Their research methodology was superior to that of Biggane and Stewart in that control groups were used to measure the performance and attitudinal effects of the changes introduced. In the case of sales representatives, the jobs of fifteen salesmen were enriched. The theme of the changes was to provide increased autonomy and responsibility for the individual. This was achieved in the following way. The salesmen were: (a) no longer required to write reports on each customer call, but merely to pass on information where they thought it appropriate; (b) authorized to make financial settlements up to the value of approximately £100 in the event of customer complaints; (c) given a discretionary range of 10 per cent on the selling price of most products; and (d) allowed to determine the frequency of customer calls. The remainder of the sales force, numbering twenty-three, was used as a control group. They did not have these four additional areas of discretion. The experiment ran for a period of nine months and the attitudes and performance of sales representatives at the end of that period were compared with their attitudes and performance before the enrichment programme. The mean attitude score of the control group did not change, and their sales performance declined by 5 per cent. The experimental group, however, reported more favourable attitudes at the end of the experiment and their sales performance increased by 19 per cent. Similar enrichment programmes were introduced for design engineers, factory supervisors and laboratory technicians. In each case there was evidence of improved employee satisfaction and higher job performance. Whilst individually each of the four studies reported by Paul and his colleagues has its limitations (for example, the statistical significance of the recorded attitudinal changes of the sales representatives is not reported), collectively they present a persuasive picture. Possibilities exist for enriching jobs of these kinds, and this can result in benefits both to employee satisfaction and performance.

Civilian employees of a military organization which serviced instruments for aircraft were the subjects of an investigation into the introduction of autonomous working-groups (Davis and Valfer, 1965). Employees were divided into 'shops', comprising twelve to thirty individuals, each of which processed relatively homogeneous types of equipment. Traditionally the work was organized in three stages. Groups first overhauled and repaired the types of equipment in which they specialized (such as flight instruments). These instruments were then calibrated and tested by a different group, and finally they passed through quality control at a third stage. In redesigning the work two modifications were introduced. In two experimental shops, the groups were required to carry out as before the first two stages of production, overhauling and repairing, but the new functions of calibrating and testing the equipment were added. This involved the operators in the acquisition of additional skills. Two control groups, matched for type of work, style of supervision, employee skills and past performance, were used to help evaluate the results. The second modification, introduced in four shops, combined all three stages of production so that the responsibilities of calibrating and testing as well as of quality control were added to the groups' functions. Quality control inspectors were withdrawn and the authority for product acceptance or rejection passed on to the supervisors of the experimental shops. Three control groups, matched on the same dimensions as for the first modification, were used. The study continued for a total of twenty-four months. The effects of both modifications may be conveniently considered together. Personnel costs, in terms of absenteeism, grievances, transfers and injuries were unaffected. Some improvement in the quality of the work was observed, and costs were reduced in the four groups to which the responsibility for quality control was delegated. Employee and supervisory attitudes improved and were favourable towards the changes made.

Rice (1958) describes a similar reorganization of work in an Indian calico mill. The installation of automatic looms in a number of plants had failed to result in the expected increases in productivity. An examination of the work of twenty-nine employees operating the automatic looms showed how jobs had been specialized and separated one from another. For example, there were weavers who kept the machines running by mending broken warp threads; battery-fillers to replenish the batteries with new bobbins; jobbers, who adjusted and tuned the looms; an oiler to keep all moving parts fully lubricated; a humidification-fitter who kept the humidity in the plant at a level necessary for the yarn to hold up in the weaving process; and so on. In all there were twelve separate jobs. Since this organization of work was proving unsuccessful it was suggested that it should be changed so that groups of individuals would be responsible for groups of looms. This involved the sharing of previously separate job assignments. Employees were strongly in favour of such a change, a fact which was undoubtedly important with respect to the subsequent effects upon attitudes and performance. Through a process of mutual choice employees were divided into four groups, each consisting of two sub-groups, one concerned with weaving, and the other responsible for maintaining the looms. The experiment was highly successful. Over a twenty-seven-month period the amount of cloth produced increased, as did the quality of the material. The attitudinal effects were equally evident, with employees being more concerned with production and more flexible in their approach to work. The changes were so successful that they were subsequently extended to the entire weaving shed and eventually to other plants using non-automatic looms. The increased efficiency of work was also reflected in higher wages.

Attempts to increase the variety and responsibility available to employees through the medium of their work have not been confined to changes introduced at the instigation of a relatively few academically orientated individuals. Several large organizations, for instance Volvo, Saab and Philips Industries, have undertaken extended projects of this nature. Philips have pursued a programme of 'work structuring' (Buitendam, 1968; den Hertog, 1975; Leigh, 1969; Pauling, 1968; Van der Does, 1969; Van Vliet, 1970). This covers the application of a variety of changes within a department. Job enlargement, rotation or enrichment have been attempted and greater opportunities for workpeople's immediate participation have been provided. Another theme is the development of small, stable working-groups, each making a product that is complete in itself.

One interesting experiment around this last theme is reported by Buitendam (1968) under the label of 'self-regulating' or autonomous groups. The main purpose of the study was to evaluate the effects of reorganizing work on a group basis. Many aspects of the work process, such as the distribution of tasks between group members, the supply of materials and quality control, were delegated to the members of the group. A daily group output norm was established and, because the greater part of quality control was transferred to the group, the number of inspection operators was reduced. The attitudes and performance of 59 employees in the self-regulating groups were then compared with those of 139 employees whose work was organized on an individual basis. Each employee in the latter group performed a separate part of the process, having an individual daily production target and having the work regulated by a supervisor. The 'self-regulating group' of employees demonstrated higher satisfaction with their jobs, had fewer complaints of feeling harassed, more positive attitudes towards their peers, but they did have more complaints about work-flow (which they organized for themselves). Communications with auxiliary departments and quality of product were also improved.

Another study illustrative of the experiments being conducted by Philips is reported by Pauling (1968, 1970). Ten women, engaged in the production of radios, were involved. Prior to the experiment the work involved the assembly of basic parts into sub-components by a group working on one assembly line, and the assembly of the sub-components into a finished product by a second group on another assembly line. One to five stages were involved in producing the sub-components, and there were five stages in the assembly of the finished radios. No job-cycle was longer than twenty minutes. The work was reorganized so that each employee was responsible for producing a finished radio from individual components, and for quality control which previously had been carried out independently. As a result of the changes the quality of the work improved considerably (the number of sets without faults increased by over 15 per cent) as did a number of indirect production costs (for instance, stock investment and the number of auxiliary staff required). The effects on employee attitudes were mixed, however. Not all preferred the longer-cycle work, though none disliked it sufficiently to take up an offer to change sections. The experiment was further extended to involve an even longer production cycle. Pauling reports that, while a careful selection of operators for this longer-cycle work was necessary, turnover was lower and there was 'lower investment in stocks, reduced supervision, greater operator satisfaction and more flexibility to meet changing demands in models' (1970, p. 8).

Other programmes have also shown that the introduction of greater variety and autonomy is not always accompanied by a change in employee attitudes. Lawler, Hackman and Kaufman (1973) describe a study of job enrichment which is particularly instructive. The participants were thirty-nine female telephone operators and their twenty-two supervisors. Part of the operators' work was modified in order to provide greater discretion in the performance and organization of work activities. That the operators experienced the changes as increases in variety and autonomy is well documented. But a comparison of attitudes before and after the changes failed to reveal any of the anticipated increases in satisfaction. Operators did not feel more involved in their work, indeed they expressed greater dissatisfaction with interpersonal relationships, and with 'the amount of respect and fair treatment I receive from my boss'. Their supervisors also registered decreases in satisfaction, especially with respect to their relationships with the operators.

Interviews conducted at the end of the experiment suggested an explanation of these findings. When operators, as part of their 'enrichment programme', began carrying out tasks which previously had been done exclusively by their superiors, the latter had a great deal of 'free' time on their hands. As a result the supervisors began to 'over-supervise' and this was not well received by the operators who felt that someone was continually 'looking over their shoulders'. Thus any positive attitudinal effects that might have resulted from the experiment were counteracted by the negative effects upon the supervisors' attitudes and behaviour. As the authors comment, the reaction of the supervisors may well have resulted from the fact that they did not participate in the planning and implementation of the changes. Additionally, no consideration was given to how the supervisors' job might be reorganized to accommodate the shrinkage in responsibilities necessarily involved. Indeed, the supervisors' job may be said to have been impoverished as a result of the changes. The dangers of focusing upon one job to the exclusion of related jobs is well illustrated by this study; so too is the possibility that the way in which changes are introduced may be as important as the nature of the changes themselves.

Numerous other studies on the effects of reorganizing work to provide greater variety, responsibility and autonomy for the employee, either on an individual or a group basis, have been reported (for example Butteriss, 1971; Conant and Kilbridge, 1965; Cotgrove *et al.*, 1971; Ford, 1969, 1973; Foulkes, 1969; Friedman, 1961; Leigh, 1969; Maher and Overbagh, 1971; Mann and Hoffman, 1960; Sirota and Wolfson, 1972a, 1972b; Weed, 1971). Useful summaries of research in this area are provided by Argyris (1973) and Birchall and Wild (1973).

The vast majority of these experimentally orientated investigations point in the same direction: the introduction of greater variety and discretion into jobs is welcomed by employees. We must not, however, allow the relative consistency of these findings to mask some important limitations. In practice, the unsuccessful experiments are less likely to be reported than those with encouraging results. And amongst the latter the evaluation of the effects of job modification has not always been entirely adequate. In relation to employee satisfaction, for instance, much of the evidence is based upon the subjective impressions of the investigators (e.g. Biggane and Stewart, 1963; Pauling, 1968, 1970; Rice, 1958), selected verbatim reports (Weed, 1971), or attitude measures which are only briefly described (Paul, Robertson and Herzberg, 1969; Paul and Robertson, 1970). Again for reasons of practicality few studies have used adequate control groups. Also, the changes introduced into jobs, and the effects of these modifications on the larger organizational system, are often poorly described. This makes it difficult to identify possible causes of observed changes in employee attitudes and performance, as does the fact discussed earlier (page 128) that re-designing jobs frequently involves simultaneous changes to many different aspects of the work situation.

Overview

In spite of these several limitations in the research evidence we are still left with the finding that most reported correlational and experimental studies in this area support the conclusion that jobs which offer variety and require the individual to exercise discretion over his work activities lead to enhanced well-being and mental health. Furthermore, the evidence shows how even extremely routine, machine-paced jobs can be re-designed to include greater variety and responsibility. Such changes are sometimes accompanied by economic benefits to the firm (through reduced labour turnover, for instance), although the smaller claim, that in simple economic terms the company is not worse off, may be more often correct. Many large and prosperous organizations have developed their own approaches to job design with such persistence that we must infer that in practical terms they have recognized its value to them and to their employees.

We should however make explicit some of the limitations of the procedures described in this chapter. They cannot serve as a universal medicine to cure any organizational illness. It is apparent for example that some jobs cannot readily be changed to increase operator well-being, perhaps because of technological constraints or because the working conditions are inalterably awful. Job-design principles of a different kind may here be more appropriate – elimination of the employee's task through automation, for instance.

The fact that payment changes will be required in most job-design exercises should also be stressed. Job enrichment requires an individual to take over additional responsibility; the discretionary element of his work is being increased relative to its prescribed content. Additional discretion is usually seen to merit an increase in pay (see page 63). The obverse of this fact presents difficulties for attempts to operate an enrichment programme in a piecework department; in order to introduce piecework in the first place, much of the employee's potential discretion had to be taken away from him, and it cannot now easily be restored. For this reason many of the more successful job-design schemes have tended to incorporate some form of measured daywork (see page 45).

Just as there are differences between jobs in their potential for enrichment, so are there major variations between people. There is little doubt that many manual workers take a largely instrumental view of their work, valuing it primarily in terms of its financial return and assessing possible improvements mainly in cash terms: the phrase 'job enrichment' may have a hollow ring to them. Others are stretched by the requirements of their work as it is, and cannot easily face an additional load, while some are simply unwilling to consider seriously any alterations to a system with which they have become comfortably familiar.

We should however draw attention to the fallacy of accepting people's initial responses to such proposals as the last word in the matter. Job re-design involves a continuing process of learning and opinion change. Several reports of altered work systems have stressed how employees influence developments, so that they may gradually come to terms with quite considerable changes in their jobs. Den Hertog (1975) summarizes a study in Philips as follows: 'One of the most important things that we learned from the experiment with autonomous groups is that work-structuring itself is a learning process in which people learn to control their own work situation, to see the system as a whole and to exercise influence in a functional way.' He notes how people's expectations and values alter in these learning situations. One group of married women employees had been loath to change from their repetitive jobs, but after a year of autonomous-group working they found it difficult to understand how they could have been satisfied with their previous arrangements. Such a change of aspiration level is regularly observed by practitioners in this field.

One practical feature which can affect the appropriateness

of attempts to re-design jobs is the breadth of variation within the group which is performing a job. If the people involved range in age from their teens to their sixties and are of widely differing intelligence, then they are unlikely to be uniformly able to accept a programme of enrichment. This suggests that varying work-methods will ultimately be required within the same department: some employees will opt for the more prescribed set of tasks whereas others producing the same item will prefer greater discretion. Further comments on this view of organizational design will be offered in the final chapter.

The attitudes of the trade unions involved are additional factors influencing the likely success of job-design attempts. It is clear that many shop stewards and full-time union officials have reservations about the philosophy behind the approach. They see that in some respects workers are being asked to take over managerial functions, a step which could threaten the traditional union role. Within parts of the engineering, mining and other industries there is still a strong feeling that working-class solidarity needs to be preserved in the face of direct and indirect encroachments by management. In so far as the acceptance of job design by subordinates presupposes their willingness to become in some respects their own managers, there exists a clear conflict of roles for many trade unionists.

Finally, the industrial relations climate within an organization crucially determines the outcome of attempts to re-design jobs according to the principles summarized in this chapter. In a sense this point subsumes all the others: if the atmosphere has traditionally been one of us-versus-them, where every move by management is viewed with deep suspicion among the work-force and where managers have little respect for their subordinates, proposals for job re-design are unlikely to get off the ground. This does not mean, however, that both management and unions should not set them up as objectives to be attained after some time: they may *first* work together to minimize job dissatisfaction and *later* cooperate on the more positive aspects of well-being.

7 Work stress

It is often argued that as society evolves, with the accompanying changes in technology, the 'information explosion', 'high-pressure living' and an acceleration in the pace of life, man is faced with ever-mounting pressures and that consequently he feels increasingly under stress. In support of this contention one finds evidence cited of an increase in illnesses recognized as symptomatic of psychological stress, such as psychosis, neurosis, nervous breakdown, coronary disease, raised blood-pressure, dyspepsia, ulcers and headaches (see Kets de Vries and Zaleznik, 1973; McGrath, 1970; Selye, 1956). Whereas there has been a 22 per cent rise over the last fifteen years in the amount of absence from work attributable to purely physical diseases, during the same period there have been increases of 152 per cent for men, and 302 per cent for women, in absence due to neurosis and psychosis (Kearns, 1973, p. 101; see also National Association for Mental Health, 1971). Whether such increases are indicative solely of increased stress is a moot point, since changing diagnostic practices or more 'enlightened' views about the legitimacy of psychological reasons for absence may also be contributing factors. Nevertheless there is sufficient evidence to warrant serious inquiry into stress at work.

We have all experienced stress in one form or another and have some knowledge of its origins and effects. In extreme situations its occurrence, causes and consequences are readily identifiable. Soldiers at the battle front, for instance, are clearly under stress. The principal cause is the threat to life and limb, and the effects are known to be detrimental not only to the individual's immediate emotional stability and behaviour but also to his longer-term psychological well-being (see Grinker and Spiegel, 1945a, 1945b; Marshall, 1947; Mira, 1943). However, situations in which the individual's safety is assured, but his interaction with the environment severely restricted, are also sources of stress. Laboratory experiments on 'sensory deprivation', where sight, sound, hearing and touch are all limited, show that lack of stimulation soon becomes unbearable to the individual and can cause hallucinations and disorientation even over relatively short periods of time (Heron, 1961; Lilly, 1956; Lilly and Shurley, 1958). Studies into the psychological effects of space travel yield corroborative evidence as do accounts of the effects of solitary confinement. Stress is clearly defined in these situations in terms of the individual's experience of tension, anxiety, fear, discomfort and associated psychological disorders.

In everyday situations, however, the sources of stress are more subtle and varied. It appears that stress occurs whenever there is a departure from optimum conditions which the individual is unable, or finds difficult, to correct. It arises as a result of too much *or* too little of situational characteristics which are important to the individual (McGrath, 1970; Sells, 1970; Welford, 1973). Thus almost any aspect of a work situation is a candidate: extremes of heat, noise or light, too great or too small a workload, too little or too much responsibility and so on. But such a general formulation is of limited practical use in increasing our understanding of stress at work. We need to know which aspects of work do in fact tend to depart from the optimum and thereby create stress. One approach to this question is based upon comparison. By identifying occupational groups with a disproportionately high level of stress and comparing them with similar occupations where stress reactions are less marked, insights concerning the causal factors can emerge.

Before turning our attention to such comparative studies, one further point remains to be made about vocabulary in this area. We are using the term 'stress' to refer to a state *of the individual* and the psychological disorders which are associated with it. 'Stressor' is a term which may be used to refer to the properties *of the environment* which are causally implicated

(Kearns, 1973). A different notion has, however, been adopted by other authors (e.g. French and Caplan, 1973; Kahn, 1973; Kahn *et al.*, 1964; Lazarus, 1966). Employing an engineering analogy, they use 'stress' to refer to the property of the environment and 'strain' as the affective reaction of the individual. We raise the alternative terminology at this juncture in order to avoid subsequent confusion and to aid the reader who wishes to look further into the subject. In practice, we opt here for the former notation, in terms of environmental stressors causing stress, as more clearly identified with common usage.

Comparative studies of stress

To introduce this examination of stress in particular kinds of work, consider the following description by a machine-minder in a knitwear factory. The job was one which many trainees could not adjust to:

Watching the cones, checking the fabric, attending the machines which constantly break down, you're on the go all the time. If a machine stops, it must be started, and when it is going the cones are running out and have to be replaced. Hour after hour without break, from one machine to another and back, putting up ends, changing cones, starting the machines and trying to watch the fabric. The machines aren't designed for the operator. You bend low to see the fabric, and climb up on the machine to reach the arms holding the thread. To see all the cones you have to walk twenty-five feet round. Usually an operative has three machines with a total of 150 cones – many of which you can't see immediately because they're on the other side of the machines; you have to memorize which cones are going to run out. With bad yarn the machines snag constantly; it's gruelling keeping everything running ...

Hey, the machine's stopped. A top red light? Find a stick, disentangle the thread – break off the balled-up yarn, put the end up, check the thread is not caught, press the button, throw the handle. Peer at the fabric – needles? lines from tight yarn? Feel the yarn as it runs, alter the tension; we're not supposed to, it's the supervisor's job but he's too busy. Change a tight cone. A red light above droppers – cone run out? press-off? A yellow light – the stop motion has come up, maybe something is out of position on the needles, a build-up of thread or a broken needle. Clear the build-up, change the needle, start the machine again. And the other machines, are they all right? One of them stops every other minute on average. Can't spend more than thirty seconds looking at one, leave it for the two others, make sure they're all right, come back to the first. May take five or ten minutes to clear. By the time the trouble's clear, another one's stopped. Break off the bad yarn, disentangle the cone, restart the machine – a few seconds later do the same again [Fraser, 1969, pp. 88–9].

The fast, repetitive, strenuous, paced characteristics of that job are clearly stressful. A more systematic record of stress in another group of workers has been reported by Ferguson (1973). Union representatives of Australian telegraphists had complained that their work led to insomnia, headaches, indigestion, peptic ulcers, high blood-pressure, heart-attacks and asthma. These claims were investigated through two sources of evidence. First, absences due to illness were examined for more than 750 telegraphists in three major cities. These absences were then compared to those of more than 800 clerks and engineers and 380 mail-sorters. Second, detailed medical examinations were made of over 500 telegraphists. 150 mail-sorters were also medically examined and used as a comparison group.

Both sources of evidence showed that neurosis among telegraphists was indeed high. 21 per cent of all telegraphists, for example, had been absent for reasons attributable to neurosis, whereas of the clerks, engineers and mail-sorters only 8, 3 and 10 per cent respectively had been absent for the same reasons. Further analyses served to clarify these differences. Among the factors found to be more prevalent for telegraphists were asthma, tremor of the fingers, chronic nasal disorders due to smoking, complaints of noise, and negative attitudes towards work. Moreover, those telegraphists diagnosed as neurotic in their medical examination not only exhibited higher incidences of psychosomatic illnesses such as peptic ulcers, indigestion, occupational cramp and chronic eczema, but also most commonly attributed their symptoms to the job being beyond their ability, to excessive noise and to monotony. In all analyses, attitudes towards work were found to be more adverse where stress was higher.

The comparisons made in this study were of necessity extremely gross, and causal interpretations are difficult to make. Nevertheless, the conclusion reached by Ferguson (1973, p. 660) is plausible. 'Stresses at the place of work were probably adequate to explain many adverse attitudes and to precipitate neurotic reactions.' In this case the causes of stress were identified as monotony, machine-pacing and highly skilled but repetitive work carried out by telegraphists in noisy conditions. These findings mirror those obtained by Fraser (1947) and others on the effects of repetitive work which were described in Chapter 6 (pages 118 to 124).

Very different occupational groups were studied in an investigation by Cobb and Rose (1973). They found stress among more than 4,000 air-traffic controllers, as indexed by the incidence of hypertension and peptic ulcers, to be unduly high. As a comparison group they used a sample of nearly 8,500 second-class airmen. The prevalence of hypertension among the traffic controllers was found to be four times higher than for the airmen, the number of new cases diagnosed in one year six times as high, and the average age at the onset of illness seven years younger. Moreover, within the sample of air-traffic controllers the occurrence of hypertension was higher for those working in high- rather than low-traffic-density stations. Similar findings were obtained in relation to peptic ulcers which were diagnosed twice as frequently among controllers than airmen and more often among controllers in high- as opposed to low-traffic-density towers. The specific work-factors responsible for the observed differences in the incidence of hypertension and peptic ulcers are open to discussion. The most likely, in that they are the primary characteristics of the air-traffic controller's job, are the close attention involved and the heavy responsibility the individual shoulders with respect to other people's lives.

Responsibility for others has been found to relate positively to indices of stress in terms of blood-pressure and blood-cholesterol levels (Cobb, 1973), and is an important ingredient of stress in many situations. A graphic illustration is provided by this surgeon:

> Being responsible . . . for somebody is an immensely solitary business. I noticed that when surgeons operated they sweated, even if the operations weren't strenuous. I wondered why this was, and found out when I did my first appendectomy alone. I had done a few with someone by my side. Inside I found pus, but I couldn't find the appendix. I hunted and hunted for half an hour – it seemed very much longer – and when I found it finally the appendix was normal. I paused for a moment before going on to find the cause of the pus, and found I was sweating. I had been doing nothing strenuous, poking around pushing loops of bowel this way and that – yet I was soaked. It is the solitude, the feeling that it is up to you alone which is the cause [Fraser, 1968, pp. 82–3].

Few jobs are quite like that, but we should emphasize how widespread at work are feelings of personal responsibility for others. Many manual employees are continually responsible for the safety or workload of their mates. Managers may take difficult decisions affecting the lives of subordinates and their families. And some subordinates on occasions feel responsibility towards their bosses. All of this is inherent in our work organizations, and it provides the basis for intermittent or continuing stress at levels which can affect physical and mental health.

Other studies have provided evidence about further sources of stress at work. The incidence of ulcers among foremen, for example, tends to be disproportionately high (Doll and Jones, 1951; Dunn and Cobb, 1962; Gosling, 1958; Pflanz *et al.*, 1956; Vertin, 1954) and the reason usually given for this focuses upon the conflicting demands which the foreman receives from his superiors and subordinates (e.g. Walker, Guest and Turner, 1956).

Experiments with animal subjects shed further light upon the determinants of ulcers. Porter *et al.* (1958) restrained two monkeys in a chair and presented them with the task of pushing a bar every twenty seconds in order to avoid receiving an electric shock. This they did on a shift basis, six hours of shock-avoidance, six hours rest. Two control monkeys were restrained in the same manner and were shocked whenever the experimental monkey failed to press the bar. The only difference was that they did not have the bar to push, they had no decision to make, no 'responsibility'. The two experimental monkeys developed ulcers, the control monkeys did not. Ulceration has also been shown to occur in rats as a result of conflict between avoiding electric shocks and obtaining nourishment (Sawrey and Weiss, 1956; Sawrey *et al.*, 1956). Other experiments with animals have been less conclusive, but, as Morgan states (1965, p. 338), 'even if results cannot always be duplicated, it seems clear that psychogenic ulcers can be experimentally produced in animals as a result of some kind of emotional stress'. Moreover, the stress has been produced either by requiring the subject to make frequent decisions where the consequences of failure were relatively serious or alternatively the subject has been placed in a conflict situation. Comparison with the correlational studies of air-traffic controllers and foremen is appealing.

Taken together these studies not only provide justification for the use of medical diagnostic categories as indices of stress, but also suggest some properties of work situations which act as stressors. Highly repetitive tasks requiring concentration under adverse work conditions, high levels of responsibility for others, and strongly conflicting demands all emerge as stressors.

Role conflict and ambiguity as stressors

A rather different approach to this question arises out of developments in role theory, and in particular through the concepts of role conflict and role ambiguity. Research into this subject has been given considerable impetus by the theoretical and empirical work of Kahn *et al.* (1964), and their approach should be considered in some detail.

The word 'role' is borrowed directly from theatrical usage and refers to behaviour which is attached to certain positions rather than to the individuals who hold these positions (see Sarbin and Allen, 1968). In society, for example, individuals play several roles such as those of mother or father, boss or subordinate, voluntary worker or member of the darts team. As Krech, Crutchfield and Ballachey (1962, p. 310) observe, 'for every recognized position there is an expectation widely shared by members of the community of what *should be* the behaviour of persons who occupy that position. What a typical occupant of a given position is expected to do constitutes the role associated with that position.' Similarly, Katz and Kahn (1966, p. 37), describing the concept in relation to work situations, state: 'Roles describe specific forms of behaviour associated with given tasks; they develop originally from task requirements. In their pure or organizational form, roles are standardized patterns of behaviour required of all persons playing a part in a given functional relationship regardless of personal wishes or interpersonal obligations irrelevant to the functional relationship.' Many factors combine to determine the role adopted by an individual in his work situation. An important influence will be the requirements imposed upon an employee by his superiors. Occasionally some of these are formally specified, as in a job description, but often will be communicated less directly, for example by praise or rebuff with respect to specific acts carried out by the individual. Other influences come from the expectations of the individual's peers and subordinates concerning his behaviour in a given position. For our purposes we use the term role to denote the behaviour expected of an employee as it relates to the particular position he holds in the work organization. The term *focal person* is used to refer to any individual whose role is under consideration, *role senders* to those people with whom the focal person interacts and through whom his role becomes specified, and *role set* to the focal person and role senders together. Fuller discussion of these concepts is provided by Katz and Kahn (1966), Kahn *et al.*, (1964), Hunt (1971), McLean (1970) and Sarbin and Allen (1968).

Role conflict has been defined (Kahn *et al.*, 1964, p. 19) as 'the simultaneous occurrence of two (or more) sets of pressures such that compliance with one would make more difficult compliance with the other'. In the terms introduced above, role conflict at work may be said to occur when a focal person receives contradictory demands from his role senders concerning what he is to do. Such conflict may arise from several sources; for instance different role senders may make contradictory demands ('inter-sender conflict'), the same role sender make incompatible demands ('intra-sender conflict'), or the focal person's occupancy of alternative roles, for example as foreman as well as shop steward, may result in conflicting expectancies concerning his behaviour ('inter-role conflict').

Role ambiguity may be defined as lack of clarity, or predictability, about the expectations associated with a given role. Its obverse is role clarity. A person whose role is ambiguous or unclear does not know what he is supposed to do; he may be unsure of the scope of his responsibilities, the circumstances under which he is free to make decisions, or the methods he may choose to fulfil his job requirements.

Both concepts, role conflict and role ambiguity, refer to a degree of uncertainty about what you are expected to do in your job. In the first case it is uncertainty in relation to whose expectations are to be met and in the second case it is uncertainty as to the nature of those expectations. The problems of uncertainty are frequently illustrated when employees talk about their jobs. For example, a salesman in a chemical company analysed his feelings in the following way: 'The manager is leaving so we're dissatisfied because we don't know what the set-up will be in the future – whether we're going to merge, who is to be responsible for what, and so on. It's uncertainty which is dissatisfying. Changes are made, you're left more or less in the air' (Wall, 1971, p. 251). In a similar vein, a foreman in an assembly plant replied to the question 'What parts of your work do you find most stressful?' by saying: 'It is people giving orders and nobody knows what the hell they want you to do' (Kahn *et al.*, 1964, p. 82).

That latter quotation derives from one of the most sophisticated investigations of role conflict in work situations. The subjects of the inquiry by Kahn and his colleagues were fifty-three focal persons, all managers or supervisors, together with their role senders – the individuals with whom they interacted and through whom their roles were prescribed. In total, 381 role senders, an average of over seven for each focal person, were involved in the study.

The first objective of the investigation was to determine, for each of the focal persons, the degree to which expectations concerning his role held by relevant role senders were conflicting. In order to achieve this, the following procedure was adopted. Each focal person was asked to identify his role senders, and to list the main activities involved in his work. He was also requested to assess his role with respect to the degree of conflict and feelings of tension he experienced. Those identified as role senders in relation to each focal person's position were subsequently interviewed. Each role sender was presented with the list of activities given by the focal person and asked whether the individual in question should carry them out in a manner different from his customary one, and whether he should change the amount of time he allocated to the various activities. The role senders' opinions about the correctness of the style of behaviour adopted by the focal person were also recorded. Finally, each focal person was approached a second time in order to obtain measures of his job satisfaction, confidence in the management of the organization and various personality characteristics.

An index of role conflict was derived from the collective responses of the role senders associated with each focal person. It was designed to reflect the degree to which role senders were exerting pressure upon the distribution of his time between various activities and his style of behaviour. In other words, the index of role conflict was a composite measure of the pressure which the role senders were exerting for the focal person to change his behaviour; note that this index was obtained quite independently of the reactions of a focal person.

Role conflict was then examined as a correlate of the experiences of the focal persons. Table 7.1, adapted from Kahn *et al.* (1964, pp. 66, 68 and 69), shows how certain affective reactions relate to differences in role conflict. The statistical significance of the differences in reactions is indicated in the third column of figures.

Table 7.1. Emotional and interpersonal correlates of role conflict

Affective reaction	*Degree of role conflict* *High* (*N* = *27*)	*Low* (*N* = *26*)	*P*
Intensity of experienced conflict	3·3	1·9	<·07
Job-related tension	5·1	4·0	<·03
Job satisfaction	4·4	5·6	<·02
Confidence in organization	5·7	7·3	<·001
Trust in senders	4·5	5·8	<·01
Respect for senders	4·2	5·9	<·001
Liking for senders	4·8	5·2	<·05
Power attributed to others	3·8	5·6	<·001
Communication frequency	3·9	5·8	<·001

We see that those people in roles identified by independent measures as involving higher conflict tend to experience greater role conflict, report stronger feelings of job-related tension, lower job satisfaction, less confidence in management, less trust, respect and liking for their colleagues, attribute less power to others, and show signs of social withdrawal through limiting their interpersonal communication. All these add up to indicate how role conflict is detrimental to employee well-being, and a source of psychological stress. Kahn *et al.* (1964, pp. 70–71) describe the findings as follows:

Contradictory role expectations give rise to opposing role pressures (role conflict), which generally have the following effects on the emotional experience of the focal person: intensified internal conflicts, increased tension associated with various aspects of the job, reduced satisfaction with the job and its various components, and decreased confidence in superiors and in the organization as a whole. The strain experienced by those in conflict situations leads to various coping responses – social and psychological withdrawal (reduction in communication and attributed influence) among them.

Finally, the presence of conflict in one's role tends to undermine his relations with his role senders, to produce weaker bonds of trust, respect, and attraction. It is quite clear that role conflicts are costly for the person in emotional and interpersonal terms They may also be costly to the organization, which depends on effective co-ordination and collaboration within and among its parts.

The significance of this particular investigation lies in its measurement of role conflict. The relatively objective assessment of the central variable adds considerably to the validity of the study. We know that the focal persons' reactions to their roles are correlates of certain aspects of 'reality' rather than of possibly idiosyncratic perceptions of reality. However, there is one important drawback in this study to the index of role conflict as it was used in practice. Conflict was originally defined as 'the simultaneous occurrence of two (or more) sets of pressures such that compliance with one would make more difficult compliance with the other' (Kahn *et al.*, 1964, p. 19; p. 147 of this chapter). At the same time the index of role conflict reflected the degree to which role senders exerted pressure upon the focal person *to change* his role behaviour. The point about this measure of role conflict is that it does not, of necessity, measure role conflict as defined. For instance, it could happen that all of the role senders indicated that the focal person should change in the same direction. The index of role conflict would register a high score for these circumstances, and yet no conflict would be apparent according to the definition offered since there was a *consensus* among role senders on the nature of the change they wanted. Had the index of role conflict represented the level of disagreement among role senders it would have been more directly interpretable. The index used by Kahn and his colleagues is appropriate for the alternative, quite plausible, view of conflict as the difference between a focal person's behaviour and the pressures exerted by the role senders. As it is we might assume that, in practice, their index provided an indirect measure of role conflict as defined, since the probability that all role senders (including subordinates and superiors) would exert pressure upon the focal person to change his behaviour in the same direction is not great. Hence the more the pressures, the greater the conflict. Whatever the status of the index as a measure of role conflict, its importance as an objective assessment of role pressure cannot be denied. Those under greater, probably conflicting, pressures to change their role behaviour also show reactions consonant with lower levels of psychological well-being.

Other investigations have yielded comparable results. Measuring role conflict in a manner similar to that used by Kahn and his collaborators, Kraut (1965) showed that greater conflict among sales personnel was associated with lower satisfaction with the job, the organization and with management. It was also positively related to job tension and the incidence of symptoms relevant to low mental health (see Kahn, 1973). The complementary approach, of focusing upon employees' subjective experience of role conflict, was adopted by House and Rizzo (1972) in a study involving 200 research, development and engineering personnel. Each respondent was asked to describe the role conflict characteristic of his own position by indicating the degree to which the following kinds of circumstances arose, 'I receive incompatible requests from two or more people', 'I have to buck a rule or policy in order to carry out an assignment'. The index of perceived role conflict obtained was found to be negatively related to measurements of individuals' satisfaction with 'the adequacy of authority', 'recognition' and 'job security'. Additionally, those experiencing greater conflict also reported higher levels of job-induced anxiety, tension and feelings of general fatigue and uneasiness.

The relevance of personality characteristics to the experience and effects of role conflict has been considered by Kahn *et al.* (1964). Two personality dimensions were found to be important: anxiety and flexibility. Anxiety-prone individuals experienced role conflict more acutely and reacted to it with greater tension than did people who were less anxiety-prone; and more flexible individuals responded to high role conflict with stronger feelings of tension than did their more rigid counterparts. It is interesting to note, however, that Kraut (1965) failed to replicate this last finding.

In summary, the findings indicate that for the samples studied role conflict is a source of potentially serious tension, job dissatisfaction, anxiety and lack of trust.

In addition to their study of role conflict, Kahn *et al.* (1964) looked at the second form of stress introduced earlier, that arising from role ambiguity. A role ambiguity index was derived for each of the fifty-three focal persons. This represented the degree to which the individual felt that his role senders made their expectations and evaluations concerning his behaviour clear to him, and the degree to which the content and scope of authority of his job were made explicit. The level of ambiguity reported by individuals was then related to their job attitudes and feelings. The results showed that those reporting greater role ambiguity also experienced high job-related tension, lower job satisfaction, a stronger sense of futility, were less trustful of their role senders and felt less self-confident. These results largely mirror those obtained for role conflict, but this is not because the indices of role conflict and ambiguity overlap since no substantial empirical relationship between the two indices was obtained. It is rather that both conflict and ambiguity have similar negative effects.

Lyons investigated the concomitants of role ambiguity among 156 nurses. Role ambiguity was measured on a short scale comprising the following four items:

> (1) How clear are you about the limits of your authority in your present job? (2) Do you feel you are always as clear as you would like to be about *how* you are supposed to do things in this job? (3) Do you feel you are always as clear as you would like to be about *what* you have to do in this job? (4) In general, how clearly defined are the policies and the various rules and regulations of the hospital that affect your job? [Lyons, 1971, p. 104].

It was found that those with higher perceived role ambiguity experienced stronger job-related tension, were less satisfied and showed a stronger propensity to leave the hospital.

Additionally, nurses who voluntarily left their jobs were found to be those who experienced greater role ambiguity.

The two studies considered above point in the same direction: higher levels of role ambiguity are associated with more negative reactions on the part of employees. A comment is required, however, on the scale of job-related tension. The measure of tension used in both instances included items very similar in nature to those incorporated in the role-ambiguity index. Two of the tension items, for instance, were: 'Being unclear on just what the scope and responsibilities of your job are' and 'not knowing what your supervisor thinks of you, how he evaluates your performance'. Whilst these items are responded to in terms of the frequency with which such circumstances worry the individual, they are so similar to items in the measure of role ambiguity that a positive relationship is to be expected. It might be more appropriate to see the relationship between the measures of role ambiguity and job-related tension as evidence of construct validity for the ambiguity measure rather than of the attitudinal effects of role ambiguity.

House and Rizzo (1972), however, in a population of research, development and engineering personnel, investigated the relationship of perceived role ambiguity with measures of job attitudes that did not include the job-tension index. Their results confirm those already considered, in that individuals experiencing greater ambiguity were less satisfied with their work (as measured on eight different indices) and were also more likely to report feelings of fatigue and uneasiness. Similar results were reported by Caplan (1971) and French and Caplan (1973). Despite the methodological difficulties noted above, the pattern of findings is consistent enough to be convincing.

As with role conflict, personality variables have been shown to moderate the relationship between role ambiguity and job attitudes. Kahn *et al.* (1964), for instance, found that individuals' 'need for cognition', a measure of tolerance of ambiguity (Cohen, Stotland and Wolfe, 1955), was important. The relationship of experienced ambiguity with reported job-related tension was considerably more pronounced among those with high need for cognition. Lyons (1971) reports a comparable finding using a measure of 'need for clarity', though supportive evidence was not provided by Korman (1971a).

Overload

Overload refers to having work to complete which is either too difficult, or of which there is too much, to carry out in the time available. Not surprisingly overload has been found to be a common complaint among professional employees (Kahn, 1973). More importantly, it has been found that those who experience greater overload report stronger job-related tensions (Sales, 1969), are lower on measures of self-esteem (French, Tupper and Mueller, 1965; French and Caplan, 1973), exhibit higher blood-cholesterol levels and show faster heart rates (French and Caplan, 1973).

This last index, a physical indication of stress, was chosen by Sales (1970) as particularly suitable for investigation in a laboratory situation. His subjects were seventy-three volunteers given the task of solving anagrams. Thirty-six of the subjects were allocated to an 'overload' condition in which, although individuals were told the anagrams would be sent at a rate appropriate to their ability, they were presented with many more anagrams than they could decode in the time allowed. The remaining thirty-seven subjects formed the 'underload' condition, receiving fewer anagrams to decode so that they would be occupied on the task for only approximately 70 per cent of the available time. The findings of the experiment complement those reported in field studies. Subjects in the 'overload' condition reported substantially higher perceptions of workload than did subjects in the underload condition, thus confirming that the experimental manipulation had a corresponding psychological reality. Whilst the productivity (as measured by the number of anagrams decoded in the number of minutes actually worked) of the 'overload' subjects was higher than that of their counterparts in the 'underload' condition, so too were their heart-rates, the number of errors they made and their feelings of tension and anger. 'Overload' subjects also reported lower enjoyment of of the task and lower self-esteem. As Sales concludes,

> the data imply that increased work loads may improve system performance on some levels – such as productivity – but that these same increased work loads may also exert deleterious influence both upon systems performance (e.g. with respect to errors) and upon individuals involved (e.g. with respect to their self-esteem and experienced tension and anger) [1970, p. 606].

A field study involving thirty-six managers and 139 non-managerial employees shows how the experimental results are mirrored in an on-going work situation (Buck, 1972). A measure of 'job pressure', or overload, was developed comprising items such as the following: 'feel my job puts me under a lot of pressure', 'my job makes me feel upset'. Overload was found, separately for managers and subordinates, to be related to indices of individual well-being. Those who experienced greater job pressure, for example, were less satisfied, more likely to feel they were 'going to have a nervous breakdown' and worried 'a lot about things related to the job', compared to their counterparts who experienced less job pressure.

Behavioural evidence for the same effect was reported by Powell (1973) in his study of colliery face-workers. Labour turnover was found to be significantly linked to the severity of the work at a particular face. This relationship was specially marked for older workers. Powell illustrates how face-workers quite clearly feel themselves to be under pressure from the requirements of pacing and continuous energy expenditure. It is apparent that overload is a characteristic of jobs at several organizational levels.

Overview

The model which is implicit in research into stress, and which serves to summarize the evidence examined in this chapter, may be represented diagrammatically as follows:

Each property of the work situation (Box A) is seen as an

environmental demand which, accentuated or minimized by the individual's characteristics (Box B), may result in feelings or physical indications of stress (Box C). The major features of environmental stressors (Box A) are now fairly well mapped out. We have described studies of overload, conflict and ambiguity which make clear their possible effects in the work situation. More general environmental influences should also be noted here.

Recent changes in the pattern of one's life can have quite a

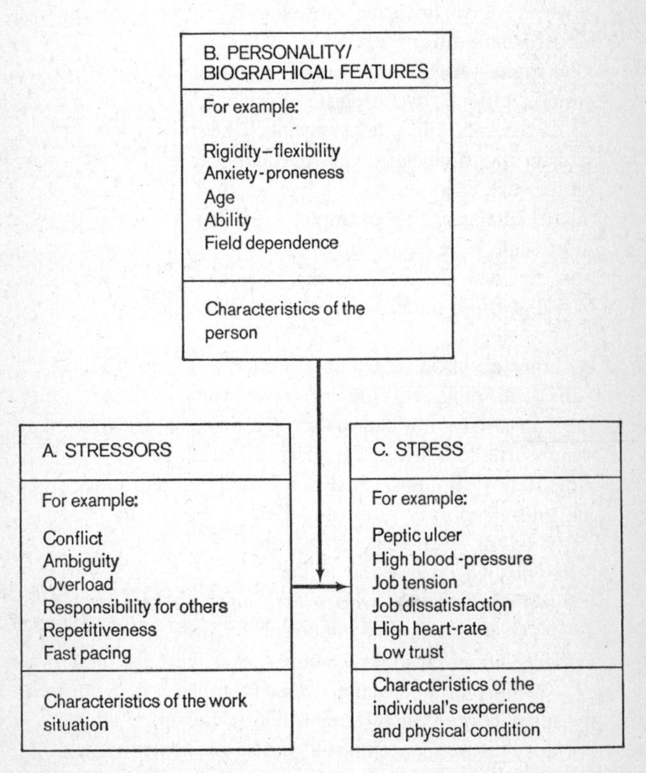

Table 7.2. Diagrammatic representation of a model of work stress (adapted from French and Caplan, 1973)

marked impact upon physical and mental health. Holmes and Rahe (1967) have described an index of recent experiences which quantifies their likely impact as stressors. This is measured in terms of 'life change units'. Death of a spouse represents the most severe change (100 units), with divorce represented by 73 units, in-law troubles by 29, major changes in eating or sleeping habits by 16, being fired from work 47 units, major change in work responsibilities 29 and trouble with the boss 23 units. Everyone experiences some life changes, so that everyone has an overall score in life change units. Higher scores do, however, show significant relationships with later illness conditions (e.g. Rahe, 1972).

This interesting finding deserves more detailed investigation by organizational psychologists. Work is one of the four areas used to classify life change events (the others are family, personal and financial), and particular attention might be paid to work events against a background of the other three kinds of changes. For example, most studies using the life change scale have been restricted to individuals who actually report to their doctor as sick; research could usefully be directed at those under stress at work but who do not report sick.

Another question requiring attention is the interaction between continuing, chronic levels of stress and temporary, acute levels. The life change scale represents an attempt to measure stressors within a relatively brief period, and experimental psychologists have conducted analogous investigations into temporary noise and heat levels or the effects of recent loss of sleep (e.g. Broadbent, 1971; Poulton, 1971). Studies of jobs reviewed in this chapter have tended to deal more with individuals who are thought to be affected by stressors continuing over long periods of time. On the basis of knowledge acquired so far we might investigate the interactive effects of chronic and acute stress. For instance, would employees in continuously stressful jobs be more affected in laboratory settings by temporary noise or heat stressors than those whose continuing work involved less stressful jobs? Such an effect, if found, would cast light on the vicious-circle aspect of stress: early stressors may make people less able to cope with subsequent ones. Conversely, an adaptation process might be found, such that regularly stressed individuals come to adapt to transient stressors.

Turning to the types of stress reaction summarized in Box C of Table 7.2, we should emphasize the fact that these are both physiological and psychological. This chapter has looked in relatively greater detail at the psychological effects of stressful work. Reviews with a stronger physiological emphasis are presented by Levi (1971). An illustration from the social-psychological literature comes from Back *et al.* (1963). These authors were interested in changes in free fatty acid levels in the blood as indicators of autonomic nervous system arousal. In the long term these levels seem to be associated with cholesterol density, and in the context of specific situations an increase in free fatty acids might provide the potential for 'fight' or 'flight' reactions to environmental stimulation. In conflict situations such reactions are temporarily prevented, and it is found that free fatty acid levels increase markedly.

The study by Back and his colleagues examined the reactions of people placed under laboratory conformity pressures, where their own private judgement was clearly at variance with those expressed by other people in the same situation. Feelings of conflict and uncertainty were accompanied by increases in free fatty acid levels. When a person resolved his conflict by deciding to publicly accept the majority opinion his free fatty acid levels tended to decrease. Once again the interaction between chronic and acute levels of this stress indicator is worth research attention.

The link between Box A (stressors) and Box C (stress) is clearly mediated by personal characteristics (Box B). We are all subject to pressures of varying kinds; some people go out of their way to find them, whereas others have difficulty coping with quite low levels. It is the fit between the person and his environment that poses the most interesting and practically significant questions for psychologists working in this field. For example, a person's general level of anxiety must affect his reactions to particular stressful situations so that people of different anxiety levels will have varying thresholds for stress. Variations will also occur which are related to ability to handle the situation and to restore it to one of acceptable tension. There are many anecdotes in managerial circles about people who have been promoted to positions where they are unable to cope with the demands of their job. This has been extended by some observers to the idea that in many organizations the majority of managers have been 'promoted to their level of incompetence'.

The personal aspects which enter into this interaction with the environment are still relatively unexplored. In addition to general notions about anxiety, ability and age, there have been suggestions that the personality dimension from field independence to field dependence might be important. This variable (e.g. Witkin, 1965) is an interesting one in terms of people's physical, social and perceptual independence of their environment. The classical test of field dependence is the Embedded Figures Test, which requires an observer to locate a simple figure in a complex design (or 'field') which is so organized as to conceal the simple figure. For some people (those who are designated field independent) the simple figure stands out clearly from its background. Others (designated as field dependent) are unable to see it even after several minutes' study.

Other features and measures of the characteristic have been investigated, including a sense of body identity and separateness from others, and preferences for personal independence in conflictful situations. Of relevance here is the apparent association between field dependence and the tendency to develop stomach ulcers (Witkin, 1965). Ulcers are found to be particularly prevalent among dependent individuals especially those who strive hard to be active and successfully independent of social supports. This effect is presumably modified by other characteristics such as type of work and ability levels.

Another personality characteristic important in the generation and acceptance of stress is achievement motivation (e.g. McClelland *et al.*, 1953; McClelland, 1961). Some people are particularly prone to set themselves targets which require personal effort and skill for their attainment and to evaluate their own performance against high internal standards of excellence. It is easy to see how this tendency may be both satisfying and stressful to the individual. People with lower achievement motivation may experience satisfaction by less stressful means.

A similar theme emerges in work on 'Type A' versus 'Type B' personalities. Several studies have drawn attention to the tendency of 'Type A' personalities to suffer coronary heart disease (e.g. Jenkins *et al.*, 1971; Rosenhan *et al.*, 1964, 1970). These people are characterized by extremes of competitiveness, aggressiveness, impatience, restlessness and feeling of being under pressures of time and responsibility. Work activities are especially important to Type A people, and they seek out stressful jobs, work long hours and meet difficult and recurring deadlines. In the study by Jenkins *et al.* (1971), for example, more than 3,000 men were followed up for about four and a half years. Of the 133 coronary heart disease sufferers in this period, 94 were identified through their earlier test scores as Type A and only 39 as Type B. This difference was statistically very significant, and found to be particularly marked for younger men. Research is now required which examines the operation of other behavioural and personality factors in conjunction with this one. The evidence presented earlier suggests that field dependence may be one of the mediators of this Type A effect.

In summary of the diagram presented on page 157 we would emphasize the need to develop interactive studies of personalities in work environments. Research into stress has made progress recently, but more complex research designs are now required. We have good outline knowledge of the work features which create stress, and we know something about the feelings and bodily changes which represent stress reactions. But we know considerably less about which people find particular situations stressful. There are clear extreme situations where everyone would be under stress, but most jobs are not of that kind: some people can tolerate them better than others. An important research question for the moment is about the differences between those who can and cannot tolerate a given level of pressure.

Related to this is the way in which people cope with stress. In many jobs people can obtain much support from colleagues (coal-mining is a notable example of this). Other aids to coping which warrant further study include withdrawal from the stressful areas or an unwillingness to take any risks. The extreme reaction may be to leave the job altogether or to take a respite through absence. Both of these responses are particularly likely among new entrants to a job, those who have not yet learned to adjust to its requirements (e.g. Hill, 1953; Hill and Trist, 1955).

Another issue concerns the intensity of stressors. We know that relatively high levels of repetitiveness, responsibility, conflict, ambiguity and workload are causally implicated in stress. However, little empirical attention has been paid to the question of whether very low levels of the same dimensions also cause stress or whether there are optimum levels of these job characteristics. It is not hard to imagine a job in which there is no repetitiveness, no responsibility, no conflict, no ambiguity and a light workload being experienced as extremely stressful, at least by some individuals.

One of the most interesting aspects of research into stress is related to the study of role conflict and role ambiguity. These concepts cut across some of the boundaries we have imposed upon ourselves in separate chapters of this book. Participation, for instance, might be reconsidered in relation to stress. We might ask how certain participative practices would relate to role conflict, role ambiguity, or indeed overload. A little evidence on this subject has been provided by French and Caplan (1973) who argue that participation serves to reduce stress by decreasing role ambiguity. The effects could, however, easily be reversed. Participative practices might raise new conflicts for subordinates; some trade unions, for example, have traditionally seen their role as one of opposition to management, and developments encouraging cooperation may introduce classical instances of role conflict. For the manager accustomed to make his own decisions participation could be a source of stress as it threatens his managerial rights and introduces ambiguity and role conflict. Similarly, some aspects of stress have implications for job design. In some cases enlarging jobs may increase role ambiguity and overload. These issues certainly deserve attention, and the point is made that the conceptual framework used in studies of stress has potential for unifying approaches to a variety of subjects, amongst which are the broad topics of participation and job design.

8 Theory and practice

In this concluding chapter we will bring together some earlier themes to summarize and extend our theoretical and practical position. It is important to emphasize that, despite a continuing concern for sound research evidence and clarity of thought, we are dealing with topics where values and personal prejudices cannot be discounted.

This became clear in the opening sections of the book, where we introduced the notion of psychological well-being at work. We were concerned with the quality of society in psychological terms and we argued that level of occupational well-being was one important index of this. Psychological well-being at work was described in terms of both job satisfaction and aspects of mental health, and our discussion of the latter was clearly about a value-laden concept. Thus we noted that Herzberg (1966) advocates as healthy an ability to tolerate and even welcome uncertainty and ambiguity; his view is not universally held. Jahoda's (1958) examination of mental health, also reviewed in Chapter 1, was based upon a recognition that what is seen as healthy can vary from group to group and from period to period. In this way, for instance, Hulin (1971, p. 174) criticizes Kornhauser's (1965) approach because it allegedly 'sees as evidence of poor mental health that members of a lower class subculture do not subscribe to middle class values'.

Our own approach clearly leads us to favour organizational change in the direction of greater employee well-being. In somewhat negative terms this may primarily involve the reduction of dissatisfaction at work, but the more positive features of well-being might be enhanced through attempts at job design of the kind described in Chapter 6. Changes may also be concerned with equitable pay structures (Chapter 3), with increased employee participation (Chapter 5), or with the reduction of stress caused by overload or by role conflict (Chapter 7). Stated in these general terms a value system favouring change in the direction of greater employee well-being is unlikely to be disputed. Granting that most readers will support the general principle, we may ask them what they are doing towards its application.

Many people in their busy organizational lives find little time for practical concern about employee well-being; their immediate priorities are elsewhere. Our major prescription must therefore be for a shift in these priorities so that more people devote more attention to the issues raised in this book. Quite clearly we cannot expect employee well-being to top everybody's ladder of priorities, but it is reasonable to urge that for most people it should become more salient in their occupational activities.

In practical terms there are two groups of people for whom this prescription is particularly appropriate – first, psychologists and other human scientists, and second, managers and trade union officials and members. Some of the topics discussed in this chapter will be of primary interest to psychologists and related workers. These appear between pages 168 and 177. The material before and after these pages is directed towards both groups.

Joint optimization

One theme which has recurred throughout the book is that there is an inherent conflict between the requirements of an organization and the requirements of its members. The successful organization is one which reconciles technological and administrative requirements with the wants and desires of its employees. This means that decisions made purely in technological terms cannot themselves be sufficient. Neither can psychological considerations always be dominant. Both are necessary for an effective organization but neither is sufficient by itself.

This line of argument is not new. It was evident in the Hawthorne studies (see pages 27 to 32) where social as well as physical factors were brought into focus, and the theme has re-emerged in many of the writings summarized throughout this book. Emery and Trist (1960) and Thorsrud and Emery (1970) are recent advocates; their emphasis has been through the notions of socio-technical systems theory (see also page 75) and the need for joint optimization of human and technological factors.

This emphasis will be illustrated here through the work of Davis (1971). He contrasts the recent 'industrial' approach to organizational design with a 'post-industrial' approach which he believes would be more appropriate. His characterization is as follows:

The industrial approach is based upon a philosophy which regards people merely as 'operating units' which may be 'adjusted and changed by training and incentives to suit the needs of the organization. That individuals may have needs is of secondary concern and, at best, simply a constraint' (p. 178). Employees are typically thought to be unwilling and unreliable, so that jobs are put together in ways which minimize individual responsibility and which have no relevance to the rest of an employee's life. (Davis notes how managers seem to regard themselves as fundamentally different in these respects.) In short, there is a widespread allegiance to the 'technological imperative'; the fact 'that a substantial part of the technical design of production systems involves social system design is little understood or appreciated' (p. 179).

The post-industrial era is thought by Davis to be swiftly approaching.

> Two trends are particularly relevant in this regard. The first is the continuing substitution of mechanical and electrical energy sources for human energy in the performance of work. The second is the absorption by machines of tasks or activities which are programmable (limited by the particular skills required for the performance of individual tasks) . . . Future human interventions will largely be of the 'nonprogrammable' variety. That is, people will be called on to provide adaptive responses in situations where there are many exceptions, or where a high degree of variability exists (making

programming infeasible), or where people provide linkages between programmable segments [p. 183].

Such a developing form of organization can usefully be viewed in terms of socio-technical systems theory, and it is the essential notions of this theory which managers, consultants and research workers should use in their discussions and plans. A practical application of this in a major United Kingdom company is described by Hill (1971). Davis's (1971) own summary runs like this:

> Socio-technical systems theory conceives of the working world as consisting of independent technological systems and social systems operating under joint causation. This leads to the central concept of joint optimization, which states that when achievement of an objective depends upon independent but correlated systems, such as a technological and social system, it is impossible to optimize for overall performance without seeking to optimize these correlative systems jointly [p. 187].

By 'technology' is meant the aggregate of plant, equipment, tools, technical knowledge and skills which are needed to achieve a certain output. The 'social system', which is closely intertwined with any technological system, is made up of people in interaction with each other. We thus reach the position where joint optimization depends upon decisions about technical and personal issues, the latter being the wants and feelings which people bring with them to work. The integration of such human factors with the more conventionally considered technological issues is an important starting point for increasing employee well-being (see also Davis, 1975).

This book has documented much that is known about some of these more important human factors, and it is clear that a great deal of knowledge is awaiting further application and extension. We have so far said little about general theories at the psychological level: granted that the operation of people's wants is of major importance, what models of this process are available? Our review in answer to this question will be of interest mainly to psychologists, and readers who are little attracted to academic theorizing may well prefer to turn direct to page 177.

Theories of motivation

Psychologists have long been interested in the nature of motivation, and it might be expected that textbooks in that field would shed light upon the occupational scene. In practice however the bulk of their research has had very little relevance to our present interests. The emphasis has largely been upon animal behaviour; and a physiological explanation has typically been the goal. The usual perspective on motivation has taken observable behaviour as primary, so that motives are seen as the hypothesized causes of that behaviour (e.g. Atkinson, 1964; Cofer, 1972; Madsen, 1961; Vernon 1969). It has been customary to claim that evidence for propositions within a theory of motivation must be restricted to statements about what someone actually does, and it has been regarded as scientifically desirable to avoid factual mention of experience and feelings.

Yet it is clear that there are experienced features of motivation which are not necessarily reflected in behaviour. People regularly want something but do not exhibit this want in action. Such a situation arises because the immediate environment only intermittently throws up a situation where choice is required, or because conflicts between wants prevent all of them being turned into behaviour.

A more satisfactory view of motivation would have to acknowledge different aspects of any motivational system. We are concerned not only with motivated *behaviour* but also with *feelings* associated with motive states. These feelings may be relatively temporary, restricted to one situation or episode of behaviour, or they may be more long term, stretching over situations and time. We can refer to these two kinds of experienced motives as episodic and dispositional wants respectively. The term 'dispositional' arises from the fact that a statement attributing some continuing characteristics to a person or object refers to a disposition to react in certain ways in certain circumstances. Thus the dispositional statement 'the glass is brittle' refers to the tendency of the glass to shatter when struck, and the statement 'he wants to be successful' refers to his disposition to think, feel and behave in certain ways in achievement-related situations.

Episodic wants are wants-in-context (see also page 20), and they are of course related to dispositional wants: someone who regularly wants to be successful is by disposition ambitious. Dispositional wants are themselves involved in attitudes and values (e.g. Audi, 1972), though we take these latter terms to be rather more broad: your attitude to pay includes many beliefs and ideas about the distribution of money in society which are not always involved in your wanting a wage increase.

Theories of motivation have typically attempted to explain why someone *did* something. An alternative question which is more appropriate in the present book is 'why did he *want* this?' Models of wanting are needed to complement the currently very restricted behavioural theories of motivation, and also because the process of wanting is central to psychological well-being at work. Several different models are available, each with its own virtues and limitations.

Instrumentality theory

A class of models examined in recent years has become known broadly as expectancy theory or instrumentality theory (e.g. Graen, 1969; Heneman and Schwab, 1972; Lawler, 1971; Lawler and Porter, 1967; Mitchell, 1974; Mitchell and Biglan, 1971; Schwab and Dyer, 1973; Vroom, 1964). In outline such a theory attempts to specify a person's feelings about different events or actions in terms of their 'instrumentality', the perceived likelihood that they will have desirable consequences. The degree to which each consequence is expected to follow behaviour is also examined, so that potential behaviour can be predicted from the expected values of possible outcomes; people are inclined to behave in such a way as to maximize the probability of getting what they want.

We may illustrate this model through Vroom's (1964) presentation. The strength of a want is defined in terms of valence, or anticipated value: 'The valence of an outcome to a person is a monotonically increasing function of the algebraic sum of the products for all other outcomes and his conceptions of its instrumentality for the attainment of these other outcomes' (p. 17). Less formally, this means that the strength of a want is a function of the attractiveness and the likelihood of the consequences of attaining that want. Research attention is thus focused on the extent to which people want consequential outcomes (pay is thus valued for what can be obtained with it), although Vroom 'allows for the possibility that outcomes may have terminal as well as instrumental value' so that, for example, 'effective performance may be its own reward' (p. 264) and a pay rise may be intrinsically as well as consequentially satisfying.

We are here mainly concerned with the valence (strength of want) aspect of instrumentality theory, but Vroom's second major proposition should be mentioned. 'The force on a person to perform an act is a monotonically increasing function of the algebraic sum of the products of the valences of all outcomes and the strength of his expectancies that the act will be followed by the attainment of those outcomes' (p. 18). In other words people are more likely to do something, the more they think it will lead to results which they want.

Research employing instrumentality theory has typically been directed to the prediction of behaviour. In addition to taking indices of behaviour, it sets out to measure possible outcomes, the valences which people attach to each outcome and the perceived likelihood that each outcome will occur. This type of approach has been moderately successful (e.g. Heneman and Schwab, 1972) and the model is valuable for its recognition that people operate in complex ways and for its attention to processes of motivational decision-making. Its major drawback in practical research arises from difficulties of measurement: people have to make a large number of subtly differentiated judgements, usually in numerical form. Associated with these problems are more basic issues about the questions which a respondent has to answer: can he in fact foresee all possible outcomes? has the investigator asked all the questions which really matter to the respondent? Statistical difficulties also abound. Should a 'terminal' value be weighted in the same way as an 'instrumental' one? Should negative outcomes be weighted similarly (but in the opposite direction) to positive ones? Should the valence score of an outcome be moderated by the perceived probability of its attainment? How stable are expectancy scores over time?

Our major worry about instrumentality theory is, however, its strong emphasis on the future rather than the present. People are alleged to think mainly in consequential terms: they want something mainly because they want the consequences it brings. A person may want £5 a week pay rise because he will later be able to buy a new car. But he wants an increase of size for other reasons as well, perhaps because his shop steward and colleagues are actively campaigning for £5. Such a reason for wanting does not easily fit into instrumentality theory: in order to make it fit, we might define a successful outcome in terms of 'getting what my shop steward and colleagues are asking for', but this approach is not entirely plausible. The sources of wanting are often much more immediate than the consequential calculations of instrumentality theory tend to suggest.

In our aim of predicting the strength of people's wants we certainly need to examine consequential outcomes, but we need also to take a hard look at more immediate sources of wanting. These will often involve comparisons with other people of a kind which are central to the next model.

Equity theory

Models of equity, exchange or social comparison have been proposed by Adams (1963, 1965), Homans (1961) and Patchen (1961). Reviews have been provided by Lawler (1968, 1971), Pritchard (1969) and Weick (1966), and we have outlined some principal features between pages 58 and 62. An early social comparison theory came from Festinger (1954), who argued that people's uncertainty about the validity of their opinions and abilities leads them into many sorts of social comparisons and activities. To check this validity they have to compare themselves with other people, either directly in social interaction or indirectly through knowledge acquired through newspapers, television and so on.

Festinger wrote primarily about opinions and abilities, but the same argument applies to people's wants. It is often impossible to evaluate the outcome of an action: how far should I be satisfied with a pay increase of £3 or with a marginal increase in consideration shown by my boss? In large measure I have to derive standards of satisfaction from other people. This means making judgements about *their* wage level or *their* boss's consideration.

So, whereas instrumentality theory stresses the attractiveness of consequential outcomes arising from an action as the basis of strength of want, equity theory emphasizes comparisons with other people. These comparisons are in terms of the rewards obtained*, but also of the inputs which different people make to their work. Thus the central question which people are assumed to ask is whether the ratio of my inputs to my rewards is similar to that of another's inputs to his rewards. Rewards are in terms of the satisfaction or pleasure deriving from pay, status, esteem, material comforts and so on; inputs refer to such features as effort, experience, skill, training, hours of work etc. The model assumes that a person will be satisfied when the ratios for himself and for others are broadly consistent; but if others are seen to be receiving more rewards relative to inputs, his wants are expected to increase. Homans (1961) views this in terms of a generally held conconception of 'distributive justice'. The rule of justice says that a man's rewards in exchange with others should be proportional to his inputs.

This approach to the prediction of wants differs from instrumentality theory in several respects. The most important difference is its emphasis on the social assessment of reward rather than upon consequential attractiveness. (The two approaches could in principle be combined, so that con-

*We use Homans's term 'reward' in preference to Adams's 'outcome' to avoid confusion with instrumentality theory employment of the latter term.

sequential attractiveness was determined through social comparison, but the benefits of integration would probably be outweighed by the complexity so introduced.) Another difference is in terms of the detailed quantitative attention the two models have received; equity theory has not been examined in so much detail in work situations, although predictions from it have been applied in laboratory studies (see page 59). But the models have in common the need for development to account for individual and situational differences. For example, the key question for equity theory concerns the identity of the comparison persons which we choose in evaluating our rewards and inputs. Very little research has been devoted to this issue.

Aspiration level

This third model is formulated in terms of comparisons with yourself at different times; the strength of wants is in part determined by the rewards and inputs to which you are accustomed. Such an idea was part of Lewin's theory of aspiration level, based upon studies of success and anticipated success in moderately difficult laboratory situations (Lewin *et al.*, 1944; see also Starbuck, 1963). A recurrent theme was the fact that task success leads to raised aspiration levels, where the latter are defined in terms of how high to set the goal for the next attempt. This fact is usually interpreted in terms of a tendency to set up higher and higher goals until success becomes uncertain: people like to enter moderately difficult undertakings, and, since practice makes these easier, aspirations tend to increase with repeated attempts.

This theme may be extended to cover wants of all kinds (cf. Child and Whiting, 1949) and can be viewed in terms of inputs and rewards. The rewards in Lewin's experimental studies were task success, but they may be any other source of satisfaction. People have rising aspiration levels for a number of reasons. Firstly, their inputs to a social relationship may well increase; the rule of distributive justice implies that in this case their anticipated rewards should also increase. A second condition is where inputs do not themselves rise. In this inputs-static condition we may still want more because we see that others' rewards are increasing: our comparison ratios are once more out of balance.

A third reason why aspiration levels tend to rise is analogous to the increases in practical ability referred to above in the summary of Lewin's research. As tasks get easier, people adapt to their present level of attainment and seek out greater difficulty. In a similar manner, as rewards become familiar, and perhaps more easily attained, people adapt to them and seek out rewards beyond those to which they are accustomed. Helson (1964) thought of this in terms of 'adaptation level', and Thibaut and Kelley (1959) wrote in terms of a 'comparison level'. As the latter authors note, 'the person adapts to the presently experienced levels: after a shift upward to a new level, the once longed for outcomes gradually lose their attractiveness' (1959, p. 98).

Arousers and constraints

Two other groups of features which affect the strength of a want may be referred to as 'arousers' and 'constraints'. Arousers increase the strength of an episodic want (see page 169) by providing reasons for wanting which are not directly connected with social or self comparisons. Constraints decrease the strength of wants, by reducing the perceived probability of their satisfaction.

Three types of arouser may be noted. The most obvious one is an environmental change which is capable of affecting everyone. In the case of pay, increases in the cost of living are of this kind; social comparisons of inputs and rewards are unchanged but wants increase. After the event we may interpret this in terms of the instrumentality of a wage increase, but the dynamic character of motivational systems is better represented by the notion of an arouser operating more directly upon the level of wanting. Another form of arouser is provided by social facilitation. Pressures within groups are of many kinds, but most can be interpreted in terms of their encouragement of members' wants. People are readily encouraged by colleagues, union leaders and mass media to want higher pay (e.g. Brown, 1973; Patchen, 1961), and the general tendency to conform to group standards of work performance (see page 76) can be viewed in terms of social influences upon individuals' wants. Lewin *et al.* (1944) have documented how social frames of reference may operate upon level of task aspiration in laboratory studies.

The notion of an arouser is also helpful in bringing the operation of personal habits within models of motivation. Habits generate anxiety in situations perceived as similar to those eliciting previous consistency of behaviour or experience. This anxiety occurs when an individual perceives a possibility that the habitual behaviour or experience may not recur. Motives aroused in this way are not easily explained through the previously described models, and they deserve more systematic research coverage. Much behaviour at work and elsewhere is of a habitual kind, with habits arousing their own feelings and wants.

Related factors affecting the strength of a want are 'constraints'; these may be defined inversely in terms of the perceived probability of getting what you want. That level of constraint affects strength of motivation has been noted by writers such as McClelland *et al.* (1953) in their discussion of achievement motivation. Both very low and very high perceived probabilities of success have lower motivational properties than moderate probabilities. This idea is also seen in the work of conditioning theorists: intermittent reinforcement schedules are particularly effective in shaping behaviour. Audi (1972) has looked at attitude systems in this light, arguing that an individual's potential for action influences the nature of his attitude, and Davis (1959) has provided formal illustrations of this process.

The present notion of a constraint as an influence on strength of wanting is that a perceived powerful constraint which indicates a very low probability of satisfaction will usually be reflected in a low level of wanting. Perceived probability is an important element in instrumentality theory of motivation, but this theory appears to assume that level of probability has no effect upon level of want. The present argument sees the two levels as determining each other.

In practice the operation of constraints can be seen in the successful administration of a national 'pay pause'; people's wants temporarily decline in a situation where they cannot be satisfied. Similarly an oppressed minority (where constraints on achievement are considerable) may be resigned to their position until they gain a first advance in freedom and privilege; they now see that progress is possible and develop more ambitious motives. The reduction of constraints is of course typically accompanied by other changes: valences may alter and different social comparisons now become relevant. And as increases in the perceived probability of success are followed by increased effort (that is, higher inputs), so are increased rewards now seen to be equitable.

Overview

In this section we have attempted to identify the main features required in a theory of wanting. We began by noting how most theories of motivation are concerned to predict overt behaviour, and our interest in the experienced aspects of motivation led us to seek models to account for the strength of episodic wants.

The three main contributors to our integrative attempt were instrumentality theory, equity theory and aspiration-level theory. Each of these approaches seems to embody some truth, the first in terms of a basic incentive value of certain satisfiers and the others in terms of recurrent social and self comparisons. But, in addition we noted how the concepts of arousers and constraints appeared to be helpful in accounting for the complexities which are met in this field.

In keeping with the prescriptive nature of this chapter it is appropriate to ask psychologists to turn attention more to the development of models of wanting. This prescription has two aspects: we need more model-building attempts to complement the recent heavy emphasis on data gathering, and we need relatively more concern with experienced wants and relatively less with exhibited behaviour. Warr (1975) has presented a more detailed review of theories in this field, relating the required features of a theory to present coverage of established models. Their major omission is seen to be in terms of the way actions are structured into sequences.

Our day-to-day life involves continuing choices of goals and sub-goals. We may want any number of objectives, but once we have made an overall choice (to complete a piece of work by lunchtime, for instance) this commitment carries with it a kind of traction which draws us along and motivates trial-and-error attempts at sub-goals. A principal aim of motivation theorists at the moment should be to understand and measure these structural aspects of wants and actions and to incorporate them into traditional theories of the kind discussed in this book.

Self-esteem and well-being

In this section we return to matters of interest beyond the limited world of research psychology. It is our experience that many managers and trade unionists are interested in talking about psychological well-being at work, but find some of the ideas obscure and confusing. This is particularly so for what were in Chapter 1 described as the more positive aspects of well-being; the more negative aspects to do with working conditions or pay are relatively easily grasped and examined.

The discussion in Chapter 1 of the positive features of occupational well-being covered such themes as psychological growth, the development of knowledge, effectiveness in ambiguity, and self-actualization. Such themes need developing and refining in the future, but for immediate practical purposes much of their significance can be captured through a focus on self-esteem. It is the individual employee's self-esteem which needs to be protected and enhanced through his choice of job and through the requirements which his employing organization imposes upon him.

Self-esteem is the evaluation which a person makes and customarily holds about himself: it expresses an attitude of approval or disapproval, and indicates the extent to which he thinks of himself as capable, significant, successful and worthy (e.g. Coopersmith, 1967, p. 5). The types of success and worth which matter to someone are a complex reflection of his personality and upbringing, but in general terms self-esteem arises from an active set of wants which are reasonably well satisfied. This view echoes those of Kornhauser and Maslow cited on pages 19 and 33 respectively, and has two important features. In the first place self-esteem requires that people have active wants: people at work who passively accept their lot and want neither to work nor to achieve other satisfactions cannot enhance their self-esteem through their employment. And secondly, self-esteem requires that to some reasonable level their wants are satisfied.

The centrality of self-esteem to individual well-being and mental health has long been recognized. Adler (1939), Fromm (1947), Horney (1937) and Rogers (1961) are among those who have argued that at least moderate self-esteem is essential for adequate personal functioning. Such importance clearly extends into the work situation. Indeed, at the risk of some oversimplification the discussion throughout this book may be recast in terms of the organizational and moral obligation to maintain and develop the self-esteem of employees. In aiming for joint optimization of employee and organizational goals, we are thus required to give greater consideration to the self-respect and self-evaluation of the organization's members.

In general terms we build up our own self-image through continuing contact with people of different outlooks and abilities, and we acquire a socially validated view of what we are capable of and what we want to attain in life (e.g. Becker, 1972). The salience of self-esteem in more specific questions of employee relations is clear in many ways. At the one extreme, to be unemployed does not merely face you with a drop in income, it also cuts you off from many of your habitual rewards and satisfying social comparisons. You may well question your own worth as a worker and even as a family provider. Repeated unsuccessful attempts to find a job gnaw further at your self-respect, and the consequences of this may spread more widely than do the consequences of mere financial deprivation.

Other illustrations of the importance of self-esteem at work come from people's feelings about their pay. We have examined in Chapter 3 how much satisfaction with current pay levels is conditioned by social comparisons. This is not merely a financial interest, it extends into a worry about your standing as a person. The level of your pay and the uses to which you put your money are important not only for their own sake, they also influence your self-esteem through comparisons with others and the operation of 'status symbols'. A related theme recurred throughout Chapter 4: we seek out social relationships in part because these can diminish our personal doubts and anxieties and can build up our feelings of worth as persons.

Chapters 5 and 6 on participation and job design repeat this theme in different ways. The central criticism of the more autocratic styles of management and organization is that they treat subordinates as organizational members who can be pushed around without regard to their feelings. Even managers who profess respect and affection for their subordinates are easily led to develop rigid organizational structures where subordinates see themselves as 'just a cog in the machine' or 'just another number'.

In analysing the nature of self-esteem the central importance of risk-taking becomes clear. Self-esteem is attained by people who have active wants of some kind and whose wants are in reasonable measure satisfied. As the discussion of aspiration-level theory (p. 173) indicated, active wants tend to increase until the probability of success reaches a moderate level: setting too easy goals represents an inactive want-system and consistently setting too difficult ones tends to reduce the intensity of wants themselves.

All levels of employees are involved in personal risk-taking. This is easy to see in the case of managers whose job necessarily requires them to weigh alternatives in an uncertain environment and to take a chance on a specific pattern of action. But in many smaller ways social interaction leads us all into risking our self-esteem; we have to take a chance that our general style of behaviour or a particular conversational theme will be well received by others. Furthermore, manual work has its own brand of continuous risk-taking in the handling of materials and estimating the consequences of particular actions. By this we do not mean that employees are continually risking accident or injury. It is more a possibility that complex work actions and decisions may prove wrong, so that the worker's efforts are in vain or not up to his personal standards. These comments from a skilled manual employee summarize the point well:

> The importance of the toolmakers' existence in the scheme of things was explained to me by many of the men I worked with. It was obviously a source of much ego-contentment and status. Each man made a complete tool, jig or punch and die by himself. While he might have to make tools based on similar principles, no two were ever the same. And since each man made the tool assigned to him by himself, with perhaps the assistance of an apprentice, he was able to lavish much self-satisfying effort upon it. Some tools which took more than a month to complete became objects of self-identification for the toolmaker [Fraser, 1969, p. 27].

An alternative way to think about the nature of self-esteem is thus in terms of successful risk-taking, where risks are acknowledged to be of many different kinds and degrees. In these terms it is a major goal of management to create organizations where people are encouraged and supported to take risks commensurate with their job level and personal ability. Such a procedure is not an easy one, since conflicts between personal goals and organizational goals are clear and since the assessment and development of personal ability require time and patience. It is however an important approach to the development of employee self-esteem.

Pursuing our analysis of this concept a little further, it seems that the idea of freedom is somewhere at the very heart of it. High self-esteem appears to arise from successful risk-taking for which the person has himself taken responsibility. Freedom to choose whether or not to follow a course of action, whether or not to take a chance, to adjust your actions and risk-levels as you proceed, all work together to develop feelings of personal worth. Membership of any social group, including a work organization, will necessarily restrict your freedom, yet too much restriction of freedom yields lower levels of self-esteem and lower intensities of want. The effects of this are not isolated and temporary; low self-esteem affects your whole repertoire of behaviour and thought.

The relevance of this theme to studies of employee participation and job design is readily apparent. It is however less obviously linked to the research into job stress examined in Chapter 7. A major feature of overload stress is that shortage of time and psychological capacity seriously invades personal freedom. In cases of stress through conflict and ambiguity, situational pressures prevent the ready movement through choices and actions that is necesssary for the attainment of goals. Buck (1972, p. 172) has illustrated this theme by contrasting self-chosen leisure pursuits like golf, bridge and racing with the constraints on activities which are met at work:

> Golf, bridge and racing are self-determined activities in which the individual has the choice of participating or not. He can decide how much self-esteem he wishes to risk in such activities and how public he wishes that risk to be. However, in industrial organizations the nature and duration of the excitation is quite often determined by others, with the possibility of damage to self-esteem being quite large. Successfully coping with today's risk may have the effect of enlarging tomorrow's risk. A failure to cope with today's risk could mean a loss of face with superiors, peers, and subordinates.

The importance of self-esteem and the easily understandable nature of the concept make it a helpful one for managers and trade unionists who are looking for a peg on which to hang developing policies in the area of well-being at work. In this respect a recent examination of the antecedents of self-esteem (Coopersmith, 1967) is worth summarizing. High self-esteem was found to develop in situations where clear and firm limits on freedom were established through rules and obligations. These constraints were however seen to be legitimate ones, wherever possible agreed rather than unilaterally imposed, and within their limits people were encouraged to make their own choices. The development of psychological well-being does not require a denial of firm management; it depends upon firm management within a context of freedom and fairness.

So what now?

We started this chapter with a general plea that increased attention should be paid to employee well-being. We followed this by an indication that joint optimization, in terms of both individual and organizational requirements, was a way forward; and that this in itself demands greater contact between those with technological skills and those with major interest in psychological questions. Theories of motivation and self-esteem are particularly required at the present time.

What other steps are needed? We should note first how dramatic the changes have been during the past ten years or so. Many new ideas and practices have found their way into discussions among managers and trade unionists, and the climate within organizations is undoubtedly changing as educational and social developments extend into occupational life. It is now generally taken for granted that people have a right to at least a basic income; and as Maslow might have predicted (see page 34) society is thus increasingly concerned about the more positive features of well-being.

A minor aspect of these developments is the increasing employment of psychologists and other professionals (sometimes called 'behavioural scientists') within organizations themselves. All this is to the good, but a particular responsibility falls upon another important group of psychologists – those employed in universities, polytechnics and other institutions of learning. These people are financially independent of management and thus extremely well placed to act as independent researchers and agents of change. They also bear a responsibility to make practical contributions to the society which supports them (Warr, 1973b, 1973c). Increasing numbers of these psychologists are turning to questions of psychological well-being at work, but there is room for much more practical concern, both from themselves and from their students.

What of the trade unions? They have clearly played a major part in raising the standards of living of their members, and will no doubt continue to do so. Their focus has however primarily been upon wages and physical conditions, partly because of the obvious importance of these but partly also because issues here are more easily thought about and measured. A shift towards the more positive features of their members' well-being would also be welcome; this might be in terms of self-esteem, as suggested in the last section. As part of this, trade unions might lead a developing resistance to over-large, impersonal work-places, and they might encourage changes in payment-by-results bargaining: instead of calculating workers' output by the hour or day, targets might be set for a four-week period, allowing flexibility and personal freedom within that period as long as the agreed target is reached or exceeded. Any other working practice with a bearing upon employee self-esteem is surely the concern of a trade union.

Personnel specialists have a clear role in these changes, but so too do engineers and accountants. In narrowly defined cost terms many of the innovations discussed in this book may seem to require additional expenditure, at least in their early stages. But in many cases this is not true, since only the more obvious features enter into the financial calculations. The costs and financial benefits of training, reducing labour turnover and absenteeism, increasing employee morale, reducing the number of disputes and so on are all inadequately measured at the present time. A total costing rather than a partial costing exercise may lead to very different managerial perspectives on the issues raised here; this deserves practical study at company level.

Furthermore, the cost *to society* of organizational procedures and characteristics is rarely recognized and almost never calculated. The social responsibility of organizations within a competitive economy is rarely of major importance to them, so that legislation may be the only way to ensure serious attention to their wider social role. This has recently occurred with respect to environmental pollution, and there is scope for parallel development in terms of psychological and social damage arising from work. The legal and organizational problems involved in the allocation of responsibility are of course formidable, and a system modelled upon industrial accident liability is not being advocated. We do however believe that governments should establish some minimum organizational requirements through which the maintenance of employee well-being can be assured.

Within management the principal responsibility for initiative lies with line managers, especially those at senior level. It falls to these people to sanction an overall policy which takes as its objective the joint optimization of employee and technological requirements. Such a policy cannot change a company's climate overnight; developments will necessarily be gradual and cautious (e.g. Foulkes, 1969). One possibility is to start in areas where there is at least a modest chance of success. In practice this means that there should be scope for technological change and there should be evidence that employees would welcome the change. Encouragement from senior management is quite essential if improvements of any substantial kind are to be maintained.

An overall policy for joint optimization will require the acceptance of flexibility in work methods based upon an assessment of what individual employees want and are able to do. There will be broad variations here; some people want much greater freedom and responsibility, others may prefer work which is straightforward and routine. Two different production methods might therefore be used side by side, with employees and management jointly deciding who should work on which. Such an idea produces horrified reactions in terms of custom-and-practice and complexities of wage bargaining when first broached with managers, but in our opinion it will certainly become more common in the future.

Associated with this is the gradual delineation of rules and procedures for joint involvement. Knowledge is slowly accumulating which suggests when and where participation in decision-making is appropriate and helpful. A blanket recommendation is valueless; what is needed is an account of those issues where superior and subordinate agree that the boss can or shall not make a decision without consulting relevant others. Again, some types of industry and people may require participative management more than others. Issues like this require research and development, but already a company's management and unions can try to specify the rules to which both sides will adhere. Employees' self-esteem depends upon realistic freedom within jointly agreed rules.

References

Adams, J. S. (1963), 'Towards an understanding of inequity', *Journal of Abnormal and Social Psychology*, Vol. 67, pp. 422–36.

Adams, J. S. (1965), 'Inequity in social exchange', in L. Berkowitz (ed.), *Advances in Experimental Social Psychology*, Vol. 2, pp. 267–99.

Adler, A. (1939), *Social Interest*, Putnam.

Adorno, T. W., Frenkel-Brunswick, E., Levinson, D. J., and Sanford, R. N. (1950), *The Authoritarian Personality*, Harper.

Aiken, M., and Hage, J. (1966), 'Organizational alienation: a comparative study', *American Sociological Review*, Vol. 31, pp. 497–507.

Alderfer, C. P. (1973), *Existence, Relatedness, and Growth*, Collier-Macmillan.

Andrews, I. R., and Henry, M. M. (1963), 'Management attitudes towards pay', *Industrial Relations*, Vol. 3, pp. 29–39.

Argyris, C. (1957), *Personality and Organization*, Harper.

Argyris, C. (1962), *Interpersonal Competence and Organizational Effectiveness*, Dorsey Press.

Argyris, C. (1964), *Integrating the Individual and the Organization*, Wiley.

Argyris, C. (1973), 'Personality and organization theory revisited', *Administrative Science Quarterly*, Vol. 18, pp. 141–67.

Asch, S. E. (1951), 'Effects of group pressure upon the modification and distortion of judgments', in H. Guetzkow (ed.), *Groups, Leadership and Men*, Carnegie Press.

Atchison, T., and French, W. (1967), 'Pay systems for scientists and engineers', *Industrial Relations*, Vol. 7, pp. 44–56.

Atkinson, J. W. (1964), *An Introduction to Motivation*, Van Nostrand.

Atkinson, J. W., and Feather, N. T. (1966), *A Theory of Achievement Motivation*, Wiley.

AUDI, R. (1972), 'On the conception and measurement of attitudes in contemporary Anglo-American psychology', *Journal for the Theory of Social Behaviour*, Vol. 2, pp. 179–203.

BABCHUK, N., and GOODE, W. J. (1951), 'Work incentives in a self-determined group', *American Sociological Review*, Vol. 16, pp. 679–86.

BACK, K. W., BOGDONOFF, M. D., SHAW, D. M., and KLEIN, R. F. (1963), 'An interpretation of experimental conformity through physiological measures', *Behavioral Science*, Vol. 8, pp. 34–40.

BASS, B. M., and LEAVITT, H. J., (1963), 'Some experiments in planning and operating', *Management Science*, Vol. 9, pp. 574–85.

BAUMGARTEL, H. (1956), 'Leadership, motivation and attitudes in research laboratories', *Journal of Social Issues*, Vol. 12, pp. 24–31.

BECKER, E. (1972), *The Birth and Death of Meaning*, second edition, Penguin.

BELCHER, D. W. (1965), *Wage and Salary Administration*, Prentice-Hall.

BELL, C. R. (1974), *Men at Work*, Allen & Unwin.

BENNIS, W. (1966), *Changing Organizations*, McGraw-Hill.

BERG, I. A., and BASS, B. M. (eds.) (1961), *Conformity and Deviation*, Harper.

BERKOWITZ, L. (1954), 'Group standards, cohesiveness and productivity', *Human Relations*, Vol. 7, pp. 509–19.

BIGGANE, J. F., and STEWART, P. A. (1963), *Job Enlargement: A Case Study*, State University of Iowa, Research Series No. 25.

BINSWANGER, L. (1963), *Being-in-the-World*, Basic Books.

BIRCHALL, D., and WILD, R. (1973), 'Job restructuring among blue-collar workers', *Personnel Review*, Vol. 2, pp. 40–55.

BLAUNER, R. (1964), *Alienation and Freedom*, University of Chicago Press.

BLOOD, M. R., and HULIN, C. L. (1967), 'Alienation, environmental characteristics and worker responses', *Journal of Applied Psychology*, Vol. 51, pp. 284–90.

BLUMBERG, P. (1968), *Industrial Democracy: The Sociology of Participation*, Constable.

BOTTOMORE, T. B. (ed.) (1963), *Karl Marx: Early Writings*, McGraw-Hill.

BOUCHER, J., and OSGOOD, C. E. (1969), 'The Pollyanna hypothesis', *Journal of Verbal Learning and Verbal Behavior*, Vol. 8, pp. 1–8.

BRADBURN, N. M. (1969), *The Structure of Psychological Well-Being*, Aldine.

BRANNEN, P., BATSTONE, E., FATCHETT, D., and WHITE, P. (1972), 'The employee director experiment – a research view', *Industrial Participation*, No. 549, pp. 24–5.

BRAYFIELD, A. H., and ROTHE, H. F. (1951), 'An index of job satisfaction', *Journal of Applied Psychology*, Vol. 35, pp. 307–11.

BRIERLY, S. S. (1920), 'The present attitude of employees to industrial psychology', *British Journal of Psychology*, Vol. 10, pp. 210–27.

BROADBENT, D. E. (1971), *Decision and Stress*, Academic Press.

BROEKMEYER, M. J. (1968), *De Arbeidsraad in Zuidslavië*, Boom.

BROWN, W. (1973), *Piecework Bargaining*, Heinemann.

BUCK, V. E. (1972), *Working under Pressure*, Staples Press.

BUITENDAM, A. (1968), *Deverticalization in Production Organizations*, Report by the Research Unit, Department of Industrial Psychology, Philips Industries, Eindhoven.

BURNETT, I. (1925), 'An experimental investigation into repetitive work', Report No. 30, Industrial Fatigue Research Board, HMSO.

BURNS, T., and STALKER, G. M. (1961), *The Management of Innovation*, Tavistock Publications.

BUTTERISS, M. (1971), *Job Enrichment and Employee Participation – A Study*, Institute of Personnel Management.

CAMERON, P., STEWART, L., CRAIG, L., and EPPELMAN, L. J. (1973), 'Thing versus self versus other mental orientation across the life-span: a note', *British Journal of Psychology*, Vol. 64, pp. 283–6.

CAPLAN, R. D. (1971), *Organizational Stress and Individual Strain: A Social Psychological Study of Risk Factors in Coronary Heart Disease among Administrators, Engineers and Scientists*, Doctoral Dissertation, University of Michigan, Ann Arbor.

CARLSON, R. E. (1969), 'Degree of job fit as a moderator of the relationship between job performance and job satisfaction', *Personnel Psychology*, Vol. 22, pp. 159–70.

CENTERS, R., and BUGENTAL, D. E. (1966), 'Intrinsic and

extrinsic job motivation among different segments of the working population', *Journal of Applied Psychology*, Vol. 50, pp. 193–7.

CHADWICK-JONES, J. (1969), *Automation and Behaviour*, Wiley.

CHERNS, A. B. (1975), 'Social change and work', in P. Warr (ed.), *Personal Goals and Work Design*, Wiley.

CHILD, I. L., and WHITING, J. W. M. (1949), 'Determinants of level of aspiration: evidence from everyday life', *Journal of Abnormal and Social Psychology*, Vol. 44, pp. 303–14.

COBB, S. (1973), 'Role responsibility: the differentiation of a concept', *Occupational Mental Health*, Vol. 3, pp. 10–14.

COBB, S., and ROSE, R. M. (1973), 'Hypertension, peptic ulcer, and diabetes in Air Traffic Controllers', *The Journal of the American Medical Association*, Vol. 224, pp. 489–92.

COCH, L., and FRENCH, J. R. P., JR (1948), 'Overcoming resistance to change', *Human Relations*, Vol. 1, pp. 512–32.

COFER, C. N. (1972), *Motivation and Emotion*, Scott, Foresman.

COHEN, A., STOTLAND, E., and WOLFE, D. (1955), 'An experimental investigation of need for cognition', *Journal of Abnormal Social Psychology*, Vol. 51, pp. 291–4.

COLLINS, B. E., and RAVEN, B. H. (1969), 'Group structure: attraction, coalition, communication and power', in G. Lindzey and E. Aronson (eds.), *Handbook of Social Psychology*, Vol. 4, Addison Wesley.

CONANT, E. H., and KILBRIDGE, M. D. (1965), 'An interdisciplinary analysis of job enlargement: technology, costs, behavioral implications', *Industrial and Labor Relations Review*, Vol. 18, pp. 377–95.

COOPER, C. L., and MANGHAM, I. L. (1971), *T-Groups: A Survey of Research*, Wiley.

COOPERSMITH, S. (1967), *The Antecedents of Self-Esteem*, Freeman.

COTGROVE, S., DUNHAM, J., and VAMPLEW, C. (1971), *The Nylon Spinners: A Case in Productivity Bargaining and Job Enlargement*, Allen & Unwin.

CROSS, D. (1973), 'The Worker Opinion Survey: a measure of shop-floor satisfactions', *Occupational Psychology*, Vol. 47, pp. 193–208.

CROSS, D., and WARR, P. (1971), 'Work-group composition as a factor in productivity and satisfaction', *Industrial Relations Journal*, Vol. 2, pp. 3–13.

CROWE, B. J., BOCHNER, S., and CLARK, A. W. (1972), 'The

effects of subordinates' behaviour on managerial style', *Human Relations*, Vol. 25, pp. 215–37.

DAVIS, J. A. (1959), 'A formal interpretation of the theory of relative deprivation', *Sociometry*, Vol. 22, pp. 280–96.

DAVIS, L. E. (1957), 'Toward a theory of job design', *Journal of Industrial Engineering*, Vol. 8, pp. 305–9.

DAVIS, L. E. (1966), 'The design of jobs', *Industrial Relations*, Vol. 6, pp. 21–45.

DAVIS, L. E. (1971), 'Job satisfaction research: the post-industrial view', *Industrial Relations*, Vol. 10, pp. 176–93.

DAVIS, L. E. (1975), 'Developments in job design', in P. Warr (ed.), *Personal Goals and Work Design*, Wiley.

DAVIS, L. E., CANTER, R. R., and HOFFMAN, J. (1955), 'Current job design criteria', *Journal of Industrial Engineering*, Vol. 6, pp. 5–11.

DAVIS, L. E., and TAYLOR, J. C. (1972), *Design of Jobs*, Penguin.

DAVIS, L. E., and VALFER, E. S. (1965), 'Intervening responses to changes in supervisor job designs', *Occupational Psychology*, Vol. 39, pp. 171–89.

DEGREENE, K. B. (ed.) (1970), *Systems Psychology*, McGraw-Hill.

DEN HERTOG, J. F. (1975), 'Work structuring', in P. Warr (ed.), *Personal Goals and Work Design*, Wiley.

DEPARTMENT OF EMPLOYMENT (1973), 'Annual censuses of employment', *Department of Employment Gazette*, Vol. 81, pp. 739–49.

DEPARTMENT OF EMPLOYMENT (1974), 'Stoppages of work due to industrial disputes in 1973', *Department of Employment Gazette*, Vol. 82, pp. 61–3.

DOLL, R. E., and GUNDERSON, E. K. E. (1969), 'Occupational group as a moderator of the job satisfaction–job performance relationship', *Journal of Applied Psychology*, Vol. 53, pp. 359–61.

DOLL, R. E., and JONES, A. F. (1951), *Occupational Factors in the Aetiology of Gastric and Duodenal Ulcers*, Medical Research Council Special Report Series, No. 276, HMSO.

DUNN, J. P., and COBB, S. (1962), 'Frequency of peptic ulcer among executives, craftsmen and foremen', *Journal of Occupational Medicine*, Vol. 4, pp. 343–8.

EMERY, F. E., and THORSRUD, E. (1969), *Form and Content in Industrial Democracy*, Tavistock Publications.

EMERY, F. E., and TRIST, E. L. (1960), 'Socio-technical systems', in C. W. Churchman and M. Verhulst (eds.), *Management Science, Models and Techniques*, Vol. 2, Pergamon.

ETZIONI, A. (1964), *Modern Organizations*, Prentice-Hall.

EVANS, M. G. (1969), 'Conceptual and operational problems in the measurement of various aspects of job satisfaction', *Journal of Applied Psychology*, Vol. 53, pp. 93–101.

FEDERATION OF BRITISH INDUSTRIES (1919), *The Control of Industry, Nationalisation and Kindred Problems*, FBI.

FERGUSON, D. (1973), 'A study of occupational stress', *Ergonomics*, Vol. 16, pp. 649–64.

FESTINGER, L. (1954), 'A theory of social comparison processes', *Human Relations*, Vol. 7, pp. 117–40.

FESTINGER, L. (1957), *A Theory of Cognitive Dissonance*, Row, Peterson.

FLEISHMAN, E. A. (1973), 'Twenty years of consideration and structure', in E. A. Fleishman and J. G. Hunt (eds.), *Current Developments in the Study of Leadership*, Southern Illinois University Press.

FLEISHMAN, E. A., and HARRIS, E. F. (1962), 'Patterns of leadership behavior related to employee grievances and turnover', *Personnel Psychology*, Vol. 15, pp. 43–56.

FLEISHMAN, E. A., HARRIS, E. F., and BURTT, H. E. (1955), *Leadership and Supervision in Industry*, Ohio State University, Bureau of Educational Research.

FORD, R. N. (1969), *Motivation Through the Work Itself*, American Management Association.

FORD, R. N. (1973), 'Job enrichment lessons from AT and T', *Harvard Business Review*, Vol. 51, pp. 96–106.

FOULKES, F. K. (1969), *Creating More Meaningful Work*, American Management Association.

FOX, A. (1966), *The Time-Span of Discretion Theory: An Appraisal*, Institute of Personnel Management.

FRASER, R. (1947), 'The incidence of neurosis among factory workers', Report No. 90, Industrial Health Research Board, HMSO.

FRASER, R. (1968), *Work: Twenty Personal Accounts*, Penguin.

FRASER, R. (1969), *Work 2: Twenty Personal Accounts*, Penguin.

FRENCH, J. R. P., JR, and CAPLAN, R. D. (1973), 'Organizational stress and individual strain', in A. J. Marrow (ed.), *The Failure of Success*, Amacom.

FRENCH, J. R. P., JR, ISRAEL, J., and ÅS, D. (1960), 'An experiment in participation in a Norwegian factory', *Human Relations*, Vol. 13, pp. 3–19.

FRENCH, J. R. P. JR, TUPPER, C. J., and MUELLER, E. F. (1965), *Work Load of University Professors*, Co-operative Research Project No. 2171, The University, Michigan.

FRICK, W. B. (1971), *Humanistic Psychology: Interviews with Maslow, Murphy and Rogers*, Merrill.

FRIEDLANDER, F. (1965), 'Comparative work value systems', *Personnel Psychology*, Vol. 18, pp. 1–20.

FRIEDMAN, G. (1961), *The Anatomy of Work*, Free Press.

FROMM, E. (1947), *Man for Himself*, Holt, Rinehart and Winston.

GAGNÉ, R. M. (ed.) (1962), *Psychological Principles in System Development*, Holt, Rinehart & Winston.

GOLDTHORPE, J., LOCKWOOD, D., BECHOFER, F., and PLATT, J. (1968), *The Affluent Worker*, Cambridge University Press.

GOLEMBIEWSKI, R. T. (1965), 'Small groups and large organizations', in J. G. March (ed.), *Handbook of Organizations*, Rand McNally.

GOODACRE, D. M. (1951), 'The use of a sociometric test as a predictor of combat unit effectiveness', *Sociometry*, Vol. 14, pp. 148–52.

GOODACRE, D. M. (1953), 'Group characteristics of good and poor performing combat units', *Sociometry*, Vol. 16, pp. 168–79.

GORDON, L. V. (1970), 'Measurement of bureaucratic orientation', *Personnel Psychology*, Vol. 23, pp. 1–11.

GOSLING, R. H. (1958), 'Peptic ulcer and mental disorder', *Journal of Psychosomatic Research*, Vol. 2, p. 285.

GRAEN, G. (1969), 'Instrumentality theory of work motivation', *Journal of Applied Psychology Monographs*, Vol. 53, no. 2, part 2.

GRINKER, R. R., and SPIEGEL, J. P. (1945a), *War Neuroses*, Blakiston.

GRINKER, R. R., and SPEIGEL, J. P. (1945b), *Men Under Stress*, Blakiston.

HACKMAN, J. R., and LAWLER, E. E. (1971), 'Employee reactions to job characteristics', *Journal of Applied Psychology*, Vol. 55, pp. 259–86.

HALL, R. H. (1972), *Organizations, Structure and Process*, Prentice-Hall.

HALPIN, A. W. (1957), 'The leader behavior and effectiveness of aircraft commanders', in R. M. Stogdill and A. E. Coons (eds.), *Leader Behavior: Its Description and Measurement*, Ohio State University, Bureau of Business Research, Monograph No. 88, pp. 52–64.

HALPIN, A. W., and WINER, B. J. (1957), 'A factorial study of the leader behavior description', in R. M. Stogdill and A. E. Coons (eds.), *Leader Behavior: Its Description and Measurement*, Ohio State University, Bureau of Business Research, Monograph No. 88, pp. 39–51.

HAMPDEN-TURNER, C. (1971), *Radical Man*, Duckworth.

HAYTHORN, W. W. (1968), 'The composition of groups: a review of the literature', *Acta Psychologica*, Vol. 28, pp. 97–128.

HELLER, F. A. (1973), 'Leadership, decision-making and contingency theory', *Industrial Relations*, Vol. 12, pp. 183–99.

HELLRIEGEL, D., and FRENCH, W. (1969), 'A critique of Jaques' equitable payment system', *Industrial Relations*, Vol. 8, pp. 269–79.

HELSON, H. (1964), *Adaptation Level Theory*, Harper & Row.

HENEMAN, H. G., and SCHWAB, D. P. (1972), 'Evaluation of research on expectancy theory predictions of employee performance', *Psychological Bulletin*, Vol. 78, pp. 1–9.

HERMAN, J. B. (1973), 'Are situational contingencies limiting job attitude–job performance relationships?', *Organizational Behavior and Human Performance*, Vol. 10, pp. 208–24.

HERON, W. (1961), 'Cognitive and physiological effects of perceptual isolation', in P. Soloman, P. E. Kabansky, P. H. Leiderman, J. H. Mendelson, R. Trumbull, and D. Wexler (eds.), *Sensory Deprivation*, Harvard University Press.

HERZBERG, F. (1966), *Work and the Nature of Man*, World Publishing Company.

HERZBERG, F., MAUSNER, B., PETERSON, R. O., and CAPWELL, D. F. (1957), *Job Attitudes: Review of Research and Opinion*, Psychological Service of Pittsburgh.

HERZBERG, F., MAUSNER, B., and SNYDERMAN, B. (1959), *The Motivation to Work*, Wiley.

HESLIN, R. (1964), 'Predicting group task effectiveness from member characteristics', *Psychological Bulletin*, Vol. 62, pp. 248–56.

HESPE, G., and LITTLE, A. (1971), 'Some aspects of employee participation', in P. Warr (ed.), *Psychology at Work*, Penguin.

HICKSON, D. J. (1961), 'Motives of workpeople who restrict

their output', *Occupational Psychology*, Vol. 35, pp. 111–21.

HILL, J. M. M. (1953), 'A note on labour turnover in an iron and steel works', *Human Relations*, Vol. 6, pp. 79–87.

HILL, J. M. M., and TRIST, E. L. (1955), 'Changes in accidents and other absences with length of service', *Human Relations*, Vol. 8, pp. 121–52.

HILL, P. (1971), *Towards a New Philosophy of Management*, Gower Press.

HINRICHS, J. R. (1969), 'Correlates of employee evaluations of pay increases', *Journal of Applied Psychology*, Vol. 53, pp. 481–9.

HOLLANDER, E. P. (1958), 'Conformity, status and idiosyncrasy credit', *Psychological Review*, Vol. 65, pp. 115–27.

HOLLANDER, E. P. (1967), *Principles and Methods of Social Psychology*, Oxford University Press.

HOLMES, T. H., and RAHE, R. H. (1967), 'The social readjustment rating scale', *Journal of Psychosomatic Research*, Vol. 11, pp. 213–18.

HOLTER, H. (1965), 'Attitudes towards employee participation in company decision-making processes', *Human Relations*, Vol. 18, pp. 297–321.

HOMANS, G. C. (1950), *The Human Group*, Harcourt Brace.

HOMANS, G. C. (1961), *Social Behaviour, Its Elementary Forms*, Routledge & Kegan Paul.

HOPPOCK, R. (1935), *Job Satisfaction*, Harper.

HORNEY, K. (1937), *The Neurotic Personality of Our Time*, Norton.

HOUSE, R. J. (1971), 'A path goal theory of leader effectiveness', *Administrative Science Quarterly*, Vol. 16, pp. 321–38.

HOUSE, R. J., and RIZZO, J. R. (1972), 'Role conflict and ambiguity as critical variables in a model of organizational behavior', *Organizational Behavior and Human Performance*, Vol. 7, pp. 467–505.

HULIN, C. L. (1966), 'Effects of community characteristics on measures of job satisfaction', *Journal of Applied Psychology*, Vol. 50, pp. 185–92.

HULIN, C. L. (1971), 'Individual differences and job enrichment – the case against general treatments', in J. R. Maher (ed.), *New Perspectives in Job Enrichment*, Van Nostrand.

HULIN, C. L., and BLOOD, M. R. (1968), 'Job enlargement,

individual differences, and worker responses', *Psychological Bulletin*, Vol. 69, pp. 41–55.

HUMBLE, J. W. (1968), *Improving Business Results*, McGraw-Hill.

HUMBLE, J. W. (ed.) (1970), *Management by Objectives in Action*, McGraw-Hill.

HUNT, R. G. (1971), 'Role and role conflict', in E. P. Hollander and R. G. Hunt (eds.), *Current Perspectives in Social Psychology*, Oxford University Press.

INDIK, B. P. (1965), 'Organizational size and member participation', *Human Relations*, Vol. 18, pp. 339–50.

JACOBSON, E. (1951), 'Foreman–steward participation practices and worker attitudes in a unionized factory', unpublished doctoral dissertation, University of Michigan.

JAHODA, M. (1958), *Current Concepts of Mental Health*, Basic Books.

JAQUES, E. (1951), *The Changing Culture of a Factory*, Tavistock Publications.

JAQUES, E. (1956), *Measurement of Responsibility*, Heinemann.

JAQUES, E. (1961), *Equitable Payment*, Heinemann.

JAQUES, E. (1964), *Time-Span Handbook*, Heinemann.

JENKINS, C. D., ZYZANSKI, S. J., ROSENHAN, R. H., and CLEVELAND, G. L. (1971), 'Association of coronary-prone behavior scores with recurrence of coronary heart disease', *Journal of Chronic Disorders*, Vol. 24, pp. 601–11.

JURALEWICZ, R. S. (1974), 'An experiment on participation in a Latin American factory', *Human Relations*, Vol. 27, pp. 627–37.

KAHN, R. L. (1973), 'Conflict, ambiguity and overload: three elements in job stress', *Occupational Mental Health*, Vol. 3, pp. 2–9.

KAHN, R. L., and KATZ, D. (1953), 'Leadership practices in relation to productivity and morale', in D. Cartwright and A. Zander (eds.), *Group Dynamics*, Row, Peterson.

KAHN, R. L., WOLFE, D., QUINN, R., SNOEK, J., and ROSENTHAL, R. (1964), *Organizational Stress: Studies in Role Conflict and Ambiguity*, Wiley.

KATZ, D. (1963), 'Survey Research Center: an overview of the human relations program', in H. Guetzkow (ed.), *Groups, Leadership and Men*, Russell & Russell.

KATZ, D., and KAHN, R. L. (1966), *The Social Psychology of Organizations*, Wiley.

KATZ, D., MACCOBY, N., GURIN, G., and FLOOR, L. G. (1951), *Productivity, Supervision, and Morale Among Railroad Workers*, University of Michigan, Institute for Social Research.

KATZ, D., MACCOBY, N., and MORSE, N. C. (1950), *Productivity, Supervision, and Morale in an Office Situation*, University of Michigan, Institute for Social Research.

KATZELL, R. A., BARRETT, R. S., and PARKER, T. C. (1961), 'Job satisfaction, job performance and situational characteristics', *Journal of Applied Psychology*, Vol. 49, pp. 311–17.

KAY, E., FRENCH, J. R. P., JR, and MEYER, H. H. (1962), *A Study of the Performance Appraisal Interview*, New York, General Electric Company.

KEARNS, J. L. (1973), *Stress in Industry*, Priory Press.

KELVIN, P. (1970), *The Bases of Social Behaviour*, Holt, Rinehart & Winston.

KENNEDY, J. E., and O'NEILL, H. E. (1958), 'Job content and workers' opinions', *Journal of Applied Psychology*, Vol. 42, pp. 372–5.

KETS de VRIES, M., and ZALEZNIK, A. (1973), *A Socio-Psychological Inquiry into the Nature and Significance of Stress Reactions in Organizations*, The European Institute of Business Administration, Research Paper Series No. 88.

KILBRIDGE, M. D. (1960), 'Do workers prefer larger jobs?', *Personnel*, Vol. 37, pp. 45–8.

KOLAJA, J. (1961), 'A Yugoslav Workers' Council', *Human Organization*, Vol. 20, pp. 27–31.

KOLAJA, J. (1965), *Workers' Councils: the Yugoslav Experience*, Tavistock Publications.

KORMAN, A. K. (1971a), 'Environmental ambiguity and locus of control as interactive influences on satisfaction', *Journal of Applied Psychology*, Vol. 55, pp. 339–42.

KORMAN, A. K. (1971b), *Industrial and Organizational Psychology*, Prentice-Hall.

KORNHAUSER, A. W. (1965), *Mental Health of the Industrial Worker*, Wiley.

KRAUT, A. I. (1965), 'A study of role conflicts and their relationships to job satisfaction, tension and performance', Doctoral dissertation, University of Michigan, Ann Arbor, University Micro Films, No. 67–8312.

KRECH, D., CRUTCHFIELD, R. S., and BALLACHEY, E. L. (1962), *Individual in Society*, McGraw-Hill.

LANDSBERGER, H. A. (1958), *Hawthorne Revisited*, New York State School of Industrial and Labor Relations.

LAWLER, E. E. (1965), 'Managers' perceptions of their subordinates' pay and of their superiors' pay', *Personnel Psychology*, Vol. 18, pp. 413–22.

LAWLER, E. E. (1968), 'Equity theory as a predictor of productivity and work quality', *Psychological Bulletin*, Vol. 70, pp. 596–610.

LAWLER, E. E. (1971), *Pay and Organizational Effectiveness*, McGraw-Hill.

LAWLER, E. E., and HACKMAN, J. R. (1969), 'Impact of employee participation in the development of pay incentive plans: a field experiment', *Journal of Applied Psychology*, Vol. 53, pp. 476–71.

LAWLER, E. E., and PORTER, L. W. (1963), 'Perceptions regarding management compensation', *Industrial Relations*, Vol. 3, pp. 41–9.

LAWLER, E. E., and PORTER, L. W. (1967), 'Antecedent attitudes of effective managerial performance', *Organizational Behavior and Human Performance*, Vol. 2, pp. 122–42.

LAWLER, E. E., HACKMAN, J. R., and KAUFMAN, S. (1973), 'Effects of job redesign: a field experiment', *Journal of Applied Social Psychology*, Vol. 3, pp. 49–62.

LAZARUS, R. S. (1966), *Psychological Stress and the Coping Process*, McGraw-Hill.

LEIGH, A. (1969), 'Making work fit', *Business Management*, Vol. 99, pp. 46–8.

LEVI, L. (ed.) (1971), *Society, Stress and Disease*, Vol. 1, Oxford University Press.

LEWIN, K., DEMBO, T., FESTINGER, L., and SEARS, P. S. (1944), 'Level of aspiration', in J. McV. Hunt (ed.), *Personality and the Behavior Disorders*, Ronald Press.

LEWIN, K., LIPPITT, R., and WHITE, R. K. (1939), 'Patterns of aggressive behaviour in experimentally created social climates', *Journal of Social Psychology*, Vol. 10, pp. 271–99.

LIKERT, R. (1961), *New Patterns of Management*, McGraw-Hill.

LIKERT, R. (1967), *The Human Organization*, McGraw-Hill.

LILLY, J. C. (1956), 'Mental effects of reduction of ordinary levels of physical stimuli on intact, healthy persons', *Psychiatric Research Reports*, No. 5, pp. 1–9.

LILLY, J. C., and SHURLEY, J. T. (1958), 'Experiments in solitude in maximum achievable physical isolation with water suspension on intact, healthy person', Symposium, Harvard Medical School, Boston.

LISCHERON, J. A., and WALL, T. D. (1975), 'Attitudes towards participation among local authority employees', *Human Relations* (in press).

LISCHERON, J. A., and WALL, T. D. (1976), 'Employee participation: an experimental field study', *Human Relations* (in press).

LOCKE, E. A. (1975), 'The nature and consequences of job satisafaction', in M. D. Dunnette (ed.), *Handbook of Industrial and Organizational Psychology*, Rand McNally.

LODAHL, T. M., and PORTER, L. W. (1961), 'Psychometric score patterns, social characteristics and productivity in small industrial work groups', *Journal of Applied Psychology*, Vol. 45, pp. 73–9.

LOTT, A. J., and LOTT, B. E. (1965), 'Group cohesiveness as interpersonal attraction', *Psychological Bulletin*, Vol. 64, pp. 259–309.

LOWIN, A., and CRAIG, J. R. (1968), 'The influence of level of performance on managerial style: an experimental object-lesson in the ambiguity of correlational data', *Organizational Behavior and Human Performance*, Vol. 3, pp. 440–58.

LOWIN, A., HRAPCHAK, W. J., and KAVANAGH, M. J. (1969), 'Consideration and Initiating Structure: an experimental investigation of leadership trends', *Administrative Science Quarterly*, Vol. 14, pp. 238–53.

LUPTON, T. (1963), *On the Shop Floor*, Pergamon.

LUPTON, T. (ed.) (1972), *Payment Systems*, Penguin.

LYONS, T. F. (1971), 'Role clarity, need for clarity, satisfaction, tension and withdrawal', *Organizational Behavior and Human Performance*, Vol. 6, pp. 99–110.

MCBEATH, G., and RANDS, D. N. (1969), *Salary Administration*, Business Books.

MCCLELLAND, D. C. (1961), *The Achieving Society*, Van Nostrand.

MCCLELLAND, D. C., ATKINSON, J. W., CLARK, R. A., and

LOWELL, E. L. (1953), *The Achievement Motive*, Appleton-Century-Crofts.
McCLELLAND, D. C., and WINTER, D. G. (1969), *Motivating Economic Achievement*, Free Press.
McGRATH, J. E. (1970), *Social and Psychological Factors in Stress*, Holt, Rinehart & Winston.
McGREGOR, D. (1957), 'Adventure in thought and action', in *Proceedings of the Fifth Anniversary Convocation of the School of Industrial Management*, MIT Press.
McGREGOR, D. (1960), *The Human Side of Enterprise*, McGraw-Hill.
McGREGOR, D. (1967), *The Professional Manager*, McGraw-Hill.
McKERSIE, R. B., and HUNTER, L. C. (1973), *Pay, Productivity and Collective Bargaining*, Macmillan.
McLEAN, A. (ed.) (1970), *Mental Health and Work Organizations*, Rand McNally.
MADSEN, K. B. (1961), *Theories of Motivation*, Munksgaard.
MAHER, J. R., and OVERBAGH, W. B. (1971), 'Enriching indirect manufacturing jobs', in J. R. Maher (ed.), *New Perspectives in Job Enrichment*, Van Nostrand.
MAHONEY, T. A. (1964), 'Compensation preferences of managers', *Industrial Relations*, Vol. 3, pp. 135–44.
MALI, P. (1972), *Managing by Objectives*, Wiley.
MANN, F. C., and HOFFMAN, R. L. (1960), *Automation and the Worker*, Holt, Rinehart & Winston.
MARRIOTT, R. (1957), *Incentive Payment Systems*, Staples Press.
MARSHALL, S. L. A. (1947), *Men Against Fire*, Morrow.
MASLOW, A. H. (1943), 'A theory of human motivation', *Psychological Review*, Vol. 50, pp. 370–96.
MASLOW, A. H. (1968), *Toward a Psychology of Being*, second edition, Van Nostrand.
MASLOW, A. H. (1970), *Motivation and Personality*, revised edition, Harper & Row.
MASLOW, A. H. (1973), *The Farther Reaches of Human Nature*, Penguin.
MAY, R. (1967), *Psychology and the Human Dilemma*, Van Nostrand.
MAYO, E. (1946), *The Human Problems of an Industrial Civilization*, Harvard University Graduate School of Business Administration.

MECHANIC, D. (1962), *Students under Stress*, Free Press.
MILLER, E. J., and RICE, A. K. (1967), *Systems of Organization*, Tavistock Publications.
MILLER, G. A. (1967), 'Professionals in bureaucracy: alienation among industrial scientists and engineers', *American Sociological Review*, Vol. 32, pp. 755–68.
MILLWARD, N., (1972), 'Piecework earnings and workers' controls', *Human Relations*, Vol. 25, pp. 351–76.
MIRA, E. (1943), *Psychiatry in War*, Norton.
MITCHELL, T. R. (1974), 'Expectancy models of job satisfaction, occupational preference and effort', *Psychological Bulletin*, Vol. 81, pp. 1053–77.
MITCHELL, T. R., and BIGLAN, A. (1971), 'Instrumentality theories: current uses in psychology', *Psychological Bulletin*, Vol. 76, pp. 432–54.
MORGAN, C. T. (1965), *Physiological Psychology*, McGraw-Hill.
MORGAN, C. T., COOK, J. S., CHAPANIS, A., and LUND, M. W. (1963), *Human Engineering Guide to Equipment Design*, McGraw-Hill.
MORSE, N. C. (1953), *Satisfactions in the White-Collar Job*, University of Michigan, Survey Research Center.
MORSE, N. C., and REIMER, E. (1956), 'The experimental change of a major organizational variable', *Journal of Abnormal and Social Psychology*, Vol. 52, pp. 120–29.
MORSE, N. C., and WEISS, R. S. (1955), 'The function and meaning of work and the job', *American Sociological Review*, Vol. 20, pp. 191–8.
MULDER, M. (1971), 'Power equalization through participation?', *Administrative Science Quarterly*, Vol. 16, pp. 31–8.
MYERS, C. S. (1920), *Mind and Work*, University of London Press.

NATIONAL ASSOCIATION FOR MENTAL HEALTH (1971), *Stress at Work*.
NEALEY, S. M. (1963), 'Pay and benefit preference', *Industrial Relations*, Vol. 3, pp. 17–28.
NEALEY, S. M., and BLOOD, M. R. (1968), 'Leadership performance of nursing supervisors at two organizational levels', *Journal of Applied Psychology*, Vol. 52, pp. 414–22.
NORTH, D. T. B., and BUCKINGHAM, G. L. (1969), *Productivity Agreements and Wage Systems*, Gower Press.

OAKLANDER, H., and FLEISHMAN, E. A. (1964), 'Patterns of leadership related to organizational stress in hospital settings', *Administrative Science Quarterly*, Vol. 8, pp. 520–32.

OFFICE OF MANPOWER ECONOMICS (1973), *Measured Daywork*, HMSO.

OPSAHL, R. L., and DUNNETTE, M. D. (1966), 'The role of financial compensation in industrial motivation', *Psychological Bulletin*, Vol. 66, pp. 94–118.

PALMORE, E. (1969a), 'Physical, mental and social factors in predicting longevity', *The Gerontologist*, Vol. 9, pp. 103–8.

PALMORE, E. (1969b), 'Predicting longevity: a follow-up controlling for age', *The Gerontologist*, Vol. 9, pp. 247–50.

PATCHEN, M. (1961), *The Choice of Wage Comparisons*, Prentice-Hall.

PATCHEN, M. (1970), *Participation, Achievement and Involvement on the Job*, Prentice-Hall.

PAUL, W. J., and ROBERTSON, K. B. (1970), *Job Enrichment and Employee Motivation*, Gower Press.

PAUL, W. J., ROBERTSON, K. B., and HERZBERG, F. (1969), 'Job enrichment pays off', *Harvard Business Review*, Vol. 47, pp. 61–79.

PAULING, T. P. (1968), 'Job enlargement, an experience at Philips Telecommunication of Australia Ltd', *Personnel Practice Bulletin*, Vol. 24, pp. 194–6.

PAULING, T. P. (1970), 'Extension of the experiment', in *Information Exchange 5*, Department of Industrial Psychology, Philips, Eindhoven.

PAYNE, R. L. (1970), 'Factor analysis of a Maslow-type need-satisfaction questionnaire', *Personnel Psychology*, Vol. 23, pp. 251–68.

PAYNE, R. L., and PUGH, D. S. (1971), 'Organizations as psychological environments', in P. Warr (ed.), *Psychology at Work*, Penguin.

PAYNE, R. L., and PUGH, D. S. (1975), 'Organization structure and organization climate', in M. D. Dunnette (ed.), *Handbook of Industrial and Organizational Psychology*, Rand McNally.

PEARLIN, L. (1962), 'Alienation from work: a study of nursing personnel', *American Sociological Review*, Vol. 27, pp. 314–26.

PELZ, D. C. (1952), 'Influence: a key to effective leadership in the first line supervisor', *Personnel*, Vol. 29, pp. 209–17.

PETTMAN, B. O. (1973), 'Some factors influencing labor

turnover: a review of research literature', *Industrial Relations*, Vol. 4, pp. 43–61.

PFLANZ, M., ROSENSTEIN, E., and VON VEXKULL, T. (1956), 'Socio-psychological aspects of peptic ulcers', *Journal of Psychosomatic Research*, Vol. 1, p. 68.

PORTER, L. W. (1961), 'A study of perceived satisfaction in bottom and middle management jobs', *Journal of Applied Psychology*, Vol. 45, pp. 1–10.

PORTER, L. W. (1962), 'Job attitudes in management: (I) Perceived differences in need fulfilment as a function of job level', *Journal of Applied Psychology*, Vol. 46, pp. 375–84.

PORTER, L. W. (1963), 'Job attitudes in management: (II) Perceived importance in needs as a function of job level', *Journal of Applied Psychology*, Vol. 47, pp. 141–8.

PORTER. L. W., and LAWLER, E. E. (1965), 'Properties of organization structure in relation to job attitudes and job behavior', *Psychological Bulletin*, Vol. 64, pp. 23–51.

PORTER, L. W., and LAWLER, E. E. (1968), *Managerial Attitudes and Performance*, Irwin.

PORTER, R. W., BRADY, J. V., CONRAD, D., MASON, J. W., GALAMBOS, R., and RIOCH, D. (1958), 'Some experimental observations on gastro-intestinal lesions in behaviorally conditioned monkeys', *Psychosomatic Medicine*, Vol. 20, pp. 379–94.

POULTON, E. C. (1970), *Environment and Human Efficiency*, Thomas.

POULTON, E. C. (1971), 'Skilled performance and stress', in P. Warr (ed.), *Psychology at Work*, Penguin.

POWELL, M. (1973), 'Age and occupational change among coal-miners', *Occupational Psychology*, Vol. 47, pp. 37–49.

PRITCHARD, R. D. (1969), 'Equity theory: a review and critique', *Organizational Behavior and Human Performance*, Vol. 4, pp. 176–211.

PUGH, D. S., HICKSON, D. J., and HININGS, C. R. (1969), 'An empirical taxonomy of structures of work organizations', *Administrative Science Quarterly*, Vol. 14, pp. 115–26.

RAHE, R. H. (1972), 'Subjects' recent life changes and their near-future illness reports', *Annals of Clinical Research*, Vol. 4, pp. 250–65.

RICE, A. K. (1958), *Productivity and Social Organization: the Ahmedabad Experiment*, Tavistock Publications.

RICHARDSON, R. (1971), *Fair Pay and Work*, Heinemann.

ROBERTS, I. L. (1973), 'The Works Constitution Acts and industrial relations in West Germany: implications for the United Kingdom', *British Journal of Industrial Relations*, Vol. 11, pp. 338–67.

ROETHLISBERGER, F. J., and DICKSON, W. J. (1939), *Management and the Worker–An Account of a Research Program Conducted by the Western Electric Company, Hawthorne Works, Chicago*, Harvard University Press.

ROGERS, C. (1961), *On Becoming a Person*, Houghton Mifflin.

ROSENHAN, R. H., *et al.* (1964), 'A predictive study of coronary heart disease', *Journal of the American Medical Association*, Vol. 189, pp. 15–26.

ROSENHAN, R. H., *et al.* (1970), 'Coronary heart disease in the Western Collaborative Group study', *Journal of Chronic Disorders*, Vol. 23, pp. 173–90.

ROSENSTEIN, E. (1970), 'Histadrut's search for a participative program', *Industrial Relations*, Vol. 9, pp. 170–86.

ROY, D. (1952), 'Quota restriction and goldbricking in a machine shop', *American Journal of Sociology*, Vol. 67, pp. 427–42.

RUS, V. (1970), 'Influence structure in Yugoslav enterprise', *Industrial Relations*, Vol. 9, pp. 148–60.

SADLER, P. J. (1966), 'Leadership style, confidence in management and job satisfaction', Ashridge Management College.

SADLER, P. J. (1970), 'Leadership style, confidence in management and job satisfaction', *Journal of Applied Behavioral Science*, Vol. 6, pp. 3–19.

SALES, S. M. (1969), 'Differences among individuals in affective, behavioral, biochemical and physiological responses to variations in work load', Doctoral Dissertation, University of Michigan, Ann Arbor.

SALES, S. M. (1970), 'Some effects of role overload and role underload', *Organizational Behavior and Human Performance*, Vol, 5, pp. 597–608.

SARBIN, T. R., and ALLEN, V. L. (1968), 'Role theory', in G. Lindzey and E. Aronson (eds.), *Handbook of Social Psychology*, Vol. 1, pp. 488–567, Addison-Wesley.

SAWREY, W., CONGER, J., and TURRELL, E. (1956), 'An experimental investigation of the role of psychological factors in the production of gastric ulcers in rats', *Journal of Comparative and Physiological Psychology*, Vol. 49, pp. 457–61.

SAWREY, W., and WEISS, J. D. (1956), 'An experimental method of producing gastric ulcers', *Journal of Comparative and Physiological Psychology*, Vol. 49, pp. 269–70.

SAYLES, L. R. (1958), *Behavior of Industrial Work Groups*, Wiley.

SCHACHTER, S., ELLERTSON, N., MCBRIDE, D., and GREGORY, D. (1951), 'An experimental study of cohesiveness and productivity', *Human Relations*, Vol. 4, pp. 229–38.

SCHNEIDER, B., and ALDERFER, C. P. (1973), 'Three studies of need satisfaction in organizations', *Administrative Science Quarterly*, Vol. 18, pp. 489–505.

SCHULTZ, G. P., and MCKERSIE, R. B. (1973), 'Participation, achievement and reward sytems', *Journal of Management Studies*, Vol. 10, pp. 141–61.

SCHUTZ, W. C. (1955), 'What makes groups productive?', *Human Relations*, Vol. 8, pp. 429–66.

SCHWAB, D. P., and CUMMINGS, L. L. (1970), 'Theories of performance and satisfaction – a review', *Industrial Relations*, Vol. 9, pp. 408–30.

SCHWAB, D. P., and DYER, L. D. (1973) 'The motivational impact of a compensation system on employee performance', *Organizational Behavior and Human Performance*, Vol. 9, pp. 215–25.

SEASHORE, S. E. (1954), *Group Cohesiveness in the Industrial Work Group*, University of Michigan, Survey Research Center.

SEEMAN, M. (1957), 'A comparison of general and specific leader behavior descriptions', in R. M. Stogdill and A. E. Coons (eds.), *Leader Behavior: Its Description and Measurement*, Ohio State University, Bureau of Business Research, Monograph No. 88, pp. 86–102.

SEEMAN, M. (1959), 'On the meaning of alienation', *American Sociological Review*, Vol. 24, pp. 783–95.

SELLS, S. B. (1970), 'On the nature of stress', in J. E. McGrath (ed.), *Social and Psychological Factors in Stress*, Holt, Rinehart & Winston.

SELYE, H. (1956), *The Stress of Life*, McGraw-Hill.

SHAW, M. E. (1971), *Group Dynamics*, McGraw-Hill.

SHEPARD, H. A. (1965), 'Changing interpersonal and intergroup relationships in organizations', in J. G. March (ed.), *Handbook of Organizations*, Rand McNally.

SHEPARD, J. M. (1969), 'Functional specialization and work attitudes', *Industrial Relations*, Vol. 8, pp. 185–94.

SHERIF, M. (1935), 'A study of some social factors in perception', *Archives of Psychology*, Vol. 27, no. 187.

SHERIF, M., and SHERIF, C. W. (1956), *An Outline of Social Psychology*, Harper & Row.

SHIMMIN, S. (1959), *Payment by Results*, Staples Press.

SIEGEL, A. L., and RUH, R. A. (1973), 'Job involvement, participation in decision-making, personal background and job behavior', *Organizational Behavior and Human Performance*, Vol. 9, pp. 318–27.

SINGLETON, W. T. (1974), *Man-Machine Systems*, Penguin.

SIROTA, D., and WOLFSON, A. D. (1972a), 'Job enrichment: what are the obstacles?', *Personnel*, Vol. 49 (3), pp. 8–17.

SIROTA, D., and WOLFSON, A. D. (1972b), 'Job enrichment: surmounting the obstacles', *Personnel*, Vol. 49 (4), pp. 8–19.

SKINNER, E. W. (1969), 'Relationships between leadership behavior patterns and organizational-situational variables', *Personnel Psychology*, Vol. 22, pp. 489–94.

SLOCUM, J. W. (1970), 'Performance and satisfaction: an analysis', *Industrial Relations*, Vol. 9, pp. 431–6.

SMITH, P. C. (1955), 'Individual differences in susceptibility to industrial monotony', *Journal of Applied Psychology*, Vol. 39, pp. 322–9.

SMITH, P. C., KENDALL, L. M., and HULIN, C. L. (1969), *The Measurement of Satisfaction in Work and Retirement*, Rand McNally.

STARBUCK, W. H. (1963), 'Level of aspiration', *Psychological Review*, Vol. 70, pp. 51–60.

STOGDILL, R. M. (1959), *Individual Behavior and Group Achievement*, Oxford University Press.

STOGDILL, R. M., and SHARTLE, C. L. (1948), 'Methods of determining patterns of leadership behavior in relation to organization structure and objectives', *Journal of Applied Psychology*, Vol. 32, pp. 286–91.

STRAUSS, G. (1968), 'Human relations – 1968 style', *Industrial Relations*, Vol. 7, pp. 262–76.

STRAUSS, G., and ROSENSTEIN, E. (1970), 'Worker participation: a critical view', *Industrial Relations*, Vol. 9, pp. 197–214.

SUSMAN, G. I. (1973), 'Job enlargement: effects of culture on worker responses', *Industrial Relations*, Vol. 12, pp. 1–15.

TABB, J. Y., and GOLDFARB, A. (1970), *Workers' Participation in Management: Expectations and Experience*, Pergamon.

TANNENBAUM, A. S., and ALLPORT, F. H. (1956), 'Personality structure and group structure: an interpretive study of their relationship through an event-structure hypothesis', *Journal of Abnormal Psychology*, Vol. 53, pp. 272–80.

TANNENBAUM, A. S., KAVCIC, B., ROSNER, M., VIANELLO, M., and WEISER, G. (1974), *Hierarchy in Organizations*, Jossey-Bass.

TAYLOR, F. W. (1911), *The Principles of Scientific Management*, Harper. Reprinted as:

TAYLOR, F. W. (1947), *Scientific Management*, Harper.

THIBAUT, J. W., and KELLEY, H. H. (1959), *The Social Psychology of Groups*, Wiley.

THORSRUD, E., and EMERY, F. E. (1970), 'Industrial democracy in Norway', *Industrial Relations*, Vol. 9, pp. 187–96.

TOSHI, H. (1970), 'A re-examination of personality as a determinant of the effects of participation', *Personnel Psychology*, Vol. 23, pp. 91–9.

TRIST, E. L., and BAMFORTH, K. W. (1951), 'Some social and psychological consequences of the longwall method of coal-getting', *Human Relations*, Vol. 4, pp. 1–38.

TRIST, E. L., HIGGIN, G. W., MURRAY, H., and POLLOCK, A. B. (1963), *Organizational Choice*, Tavistock Publications.

TURNER, A. N., and LAWRENCE, P. R. (1965), *Industrial Jobs and the Worker*, Harvard University Press.

US DEPARTMENT OF HEALTH, EDUCATION AND WELFARE (1973), *Work in America*, Massachusetts Institute of Technology Press.

VAN COTT, H. P., and KINCADE, R. G. (eds.) (1972), *Human Engineering Guide to Equipment Design*, American Institute for Research.

VAN DER DOES, J. L. J. M. (1969), 'Work structuring: A summary of experiments at Philips – 1963–1968', N. V. Philips Gloeilampenfabrieken.

VAN VLIET, A. (1970), 'A work structuring experiment in television assembly', N. V. Philips, J. E. O. Special, No. 5.

VAN ZELST, R. H. (1952), 'Sociometrically selected work teams increase production', *Personnel Psychology*, Vol. 9, pp. 175–85.

VERNON, M. D. (1969), *Human Motivation*, Cambridge University Press.

VERTIN, P. G. (1954), 'Bedrijfsgeneeskundige aspecten van het ulcer pepticum', Thesis, Gronigen, Hermes, Eindhoven.

VROOM, V. H. (1959), 'Some personality determinants of the effects of participation', *Journal of Abnormal and Social Psychology*, Vol. 59, pp. 322–7.

VROOM, V. H. (1964), *Work and Motivation*, Wiley.

VROOM, V. H., and MANN, F. C. (1960), 'Leader authoritarianism and employee attitudes', *Personnel Psychology*, Vol. 13, pp. 125–40.

WALKER, C. R., and GUEST, R. H. (1952), *The Man on the Assembly Line*, Harvard University Press.

WALKER, C. R., GUEST, R. H., and TURNER, A. N. (1956), *The Foreman on the Assembly Line*, Harvard University Press.

WALKER, K. F. (1967), 'Workers' participation in management', *International Institute for Labour Studies Bulletin*, Vol. 2, pp. 1–62.

WALKER, K. F. (1972), 'Worker participation in management', *Monthly Journal of the Bureau of Public Enterprises*, Ministry of Finance, New Delhi, Lok Udyog, Vol. 5, pp. 1173–87.

WALL, T. D. (1971), 'The perceived determinants of job satisfaction and job dissatisfaction in a chemical firm', Doctoral Thesis, University of Nottingham.

WALL, T. D. (1972), 'Overall job satisfaction in relation to "social desirability", age, length of employment, and social class', *British Journal of Social and Clinical Psychology*, Vol. 11, pp. 79–81.

WALL, T. D., and STEPHENSON, G. M. (1970), 'Herzberg's two-factor theory of job attitudes: a critical evaluation and some fresh evidence', *Industrial Relations Journal*, Vol. 1, pp. 41–65.

WALTON, R. E., and MCKERSIE, R. B. (1965), *A Behavioral Theory of Labor Negotiations*, McGraw-Hill.

WANOUS, J. P., and LAWLER, E. E. (1972), 'Measurement and meaning of job satisfaction', *Journal of Applied Psychology*, Vol. 56, pp. 95–105.

WARR, P. (ed.) (1971a), *Psychology at Work*, Penguin.

WARR, P. (1971b) 'Pollyanna's personal judgments', *European Journal of Social Psychology*, Vol. 1, pp. 327–38.

WARR, P. (1973a), *Psychology and Collective Bargaining*, Hutchinson.

WARR, P. (1973b), 'Towards a more human psychology', *Bulletin of the British Psychological Society*, Vol. 26, pp. 1–8.

WARR, P. (1973c), 'Better working lives: a university psychologist's view', *Occupational Psychology*, Vol. 47, pp. 15–22.

WARR, P. (1975), 'Theories of motivation', in P. Warr (ed.), *Personal Goals and Work Design*, Wiley.

WARR, P., and ROUTLEDGE, T. (1969), 'An opinion scale for the study of managers' job satisfaction', *Occupational Psychology*, Vol. 43, pp. 95–109.

WEBER, M. (1947), *The Theory of Social and Economic Organization*, Free Press.

WEED, E. D., (1971), 'Job enrichment cleans up at Texas Instruments', in J. R. Maher (ed.), *New Perspectives in Job Enrichment*, Van Nostrand.

WEICK, K. E. (1966), 'The concept of equity in the perception of pay', *Administrative Science Quarterly*, Vol. 11, pp. 414–39.

WEINER, B. (1972), *Theories of Motivation: from Mechanism to Cognition*, Markham.

WELFORD, A. T. (1973), 'Stress and performance', *Ergonomics*, Vol. 16, pp. 567–80.

WESCHLER, I. R., KAHANE, M., and TANNENBAUM, R. (1952), 'Job satisfaction, productivity and morale: a case study', *Occupational Psychology*, Vol. 26, pp. 1–14.

WHITE, J. K., and RUH, R. A. (1973), 'Effects of personal values on the relationship between participation and job attitudes', *Administrative Science Quarterly*, Vol. 18, pp. 506–14.

WHYTE, W. F. (1955), *Money and Motivation: An Analysis of Incentives in Industry*, Harper & Row.

WICKER, A. W. (1969), 'Attitudes versus action: the relationship of verbal and overt behavioral responses to attitude objects', *Journal of Social Issues*, Vol. 25, pp. 41–78.

WICKER, A. W., MCGRATH, J. E., and ARMSTRONG, G. E. (1972), 'Organization size and behavior setting capacity as determinants of member participation', *Behavioral Science*, Vol. 17, pp. 499–513.

WILD, R. (1970), 'Job design research', Management Centre of the University of Bradford, England.

WILSON, N. A. B. (1973), *On the Quality of Working Life*,

Department of Employment Manpower Paper Number 7, HMSO.

WITKIN, H. A. (1965), 'Psychological differentiation and forms of pathology', *Journal of Abnormal Psychology*, Vol. 70, pp. 317–36.

WYATT, S., and OGDEN, D. A. (1924), *On the Extent and Effects of Variety and Uniformity in Repetitive Work*, Report No. 26, Industrial Fatigue Research Board, HMSO.

WYATT, S., FRASER, J. A., and STOCK, F. G. L. (1928), *The Comparative Effects of Variety and Uniformity in Work*, Report No. 52, Industrial Fatigue Research Board, HMSO.

ZALEZNIK, A., CHRISTENSEN, C. R., and ROETHLISBERGER, F. J. (1958), *The Motivation, Productivity and Satisfaction of Workers: A Prediction Study*, Harvard University Graduate School of Business Administration.

Author Index

Subject Index

More about Penguins and Pelicans

Penguinews, which appears every month, contains details of all the new books issued by Penguins as they are published. From time to time it is supplemented by *Penguins in Print*, which is a complete list of all titles available. (There are some five thousand of these.)

A specimen copy of *Penguinews* will be sent to you free on request. For a year's issues (including the complete lists) please send 50p if you live in the British Isles, or 75p if you live elsewhere. Just write to Dept EP, Penguin Books Ltd, Harmondsworth, Middlesex, enclosing a cheque or postal order, and your name will be added to the mailing list.

In the U.S.A.: For a complete list of books available from Penguin in the United States write to Dept CS, Penguin Books Inc., 7110 Ambassador Road, Baltimore, Maryland 21207.

In Canada: For a complete list of books available from Penguin in Canada write to Penguin Books Canada Ltd, 41 Steelcase Road West, Markham, Ontario